"A bold, refreshing, and funny look at the lack of leadership in the corporate world that is, unfortunately, all too prevalent."

—**R. PAUL VUOLLE**, author of *Lead Now, Manage Later: The Straight Shooter's Guide to Business Success*

"Dan Bozung's story is funny and, at the same time, poignant. It is a remarkable story of opportunity, wins, losses, and many lessons learned as Dan shares his quest to find his way in corporate America."

—**TED STUDDARD**, US Marine Corps (retired), author of *Depot to Depot*

"Hammer, meet nail. Bang! Dan's book should be required reading for anyone leaving military service. Excellent story telling with spot-on lessons learned at the end of each chapter."

—**KELLY GALVIN**, US Army (retired), author of *PowerPoint Ranger: My Iraq War Logs*

"Great read. Hilarious . . . and, yes . . . informative. A fast-paced, enjoyable page-turner. Bozung's misadventures in the corporate world should be required reading for all who leave the service. This book should be in every PX around the world."

—**CLAY CUSTEAD**, author of *From the Farm to Arlington*

"An insightful, highly engaging piece of self-analysis, in which the author makes neither excuses nor apologies. Would that we all have the courage to do this."

—**EDWARD W. BEAL**, MD, Clinical Professor of Psychiatry, Georgetown University School of Medicine, author of *War Stories from the Forgotten Soldiers*

This Civilian Sh*t Is Hard:
From the Cockpit, Cubicle, and Beyond

by Dan Bozung

© Copyright 2020 Dan Bozung

ISBN 978-1-64663-152-0

Published by

◤ köehlerbooks™

3705 Shore Drive
Virginia Beach, VA 23455
800-435-4811
www.koehlerbooks.com

This Civilian Sh*t is Hard

FROM THE COCKPIT, CUBICLE,
AND BEYOND

Dan Bozung

VIRGINIA BEACH
CAPE CHARLES

This book is dedicated to all military spouses and children.

You bear the burdens. You make the sacrifices.

You are true heroes.

For reasons I think will be obvious, most of the names in this book are not real.

And, while I endeavored to capture conversations and events as accurately as possible, I may not have gotten it all exactly right. But I stayed as true to the *spirit* of such things as I was able.

Hey, give me a break. Some of this stuff happened more than twenty years ago.

Contents

Introduction

I compiled a loose collection of stories through the years about a bunch of weird stuff I experienced at work. I had no idea what any of it meant or, taken together, what purpose it might serve. So, I put the question to a few close friends. What *is* this?

"Maybe it's a memoir. Maybe it's a self-help book. Maybe it's something about leadership or business strategy." My friends were a little unclear on what form the compilation might take. But one piece of feedback was consistent: "Wow. I had no idea you were such an asshole."

Asshole? I got defensive. "What are you talking about? Where do you get 'asshole'? I'm one of the nicest guys I know."

"You seem like the Dan I know when you talk about the Navy. But as soon as you start talking about one of your civilian experiences, you sound like a self-important, elitist, know-it-all prick."

Ouch. Tough feedback. But these were people who knew me well, so I had to at least consider its validity.

Whatever form this compilation took, I wanted it to be honest, first and foremost. And if these stories painted an honest picture of a complete asshole, I had to accept that.

Okay, I'm an asshole. Or at least, I was. Why?

I was a bitter, frustrated man. The success I so easily enjoyed in the Navy completely eluded me in the private sector. There were many causes, including an epic collision of unrealistic expectations, poor choices, and bad luck. And my resulting inability to find my groove as a civilian gnawed at me day after day, week after week, year after year. How could someone with every possible advantage upon entering the corporate world proceed to fuck it up so badly? With all of the shame and guilt I carried around, it's no wonder people perceived me to be an asshole.

By contrast, my Navy experience had consistently exceeded my expectations. I enjoyed an uninterrupted streak of excellent choices and good luck for years.

I joined right out of high school. My parents had been clear about college for as long as I could remember: "There are too many of you kids, and we can't pay for it. You're on your own."

When I discovered in the spring of my senior year that they were serious, I had to scramble to get my shit together. I had an acceptance letter to Michigan State, but not a dime saved to pay for a single textbook. As graduation loomed, all I knew was that I couldn't stick around my small town a day longer than was absolutely necessary—I was too vain for that. So off I went to the recruiting office and signed up on the spot.

I assumed the military transition would be difficult. After I got over the bad haircut and initial shell shock of basic training, it was anything but. Yes, there was a lot of yelling and marching and all that, but I quickly became accustomed to it. It was the new normal. And when I found out I had to fold my underwear a certain way, make my bed according to exact specifications, and wear my uniform in accordance with a thick, detailed manual, I welcomed it. Why? Because I discovered in bootcamp I was mildly obsessive-compulsive. I had been folding, tucking, polishing, and combing with exacting precision my entire life. It came perfectly naturally to me. *Wow! That is a* fantastic *way to fold a tee shirt. Look . . . no wrinkles!* It was almost easy.

And when I left boot camp and got to the fleet, I found people who held the same standards, who looked at the world in the same manner, and valued all of the same things I held most important. Those included hard work, honesty, and a well-stocked bar. The Navy was more than a job or a simple detour on the way to college. It was my family. It was my identity. Unbeknownst to me for the first seventeen years of my life, I'd been born to be a sailor.

My performance in the enlisted ranks earned me an appointment to the Naval Academy. And graduation from Annapolis bought me a ticket to flight school, where I earned the coveted Wings of Gold. And, with those wings on my chest, I enjoyed some of the most amazing experiences I'd ever had in my life.

And then I left the Navy, expecting my winning streak to continue, no matter where I landed. But my luck quickly ran out. I didn't know the first damn thing about being a civilian. The poor choices I made and opportunities I squandered came as a direct result.

So why did I leave the Navy? Basically, I was looking for new mountains to climb and was accepted to one of the most elite business education programs in the world—Harvard Business School. I expected amazing opportunities to always be readily available, a simple phone call to a fellow alumnus away. I expected to work hard, retire early, and then occupy seats on various corporate boards and an occasional ambassadorship. Yes, it would all be rainbows and sunshine. How could I possibly miss?

What follows is what actually happened. These are the most meaningful moments from the Navy life that shaped me and the civilian experience that nearly ruined me.

This is the story of how I became such an asshole. And these are the lessons I needed to learn to get over myself and eventually stop being one.

One-Below for Headwork

"I don't know who that joker was, but I got his number!"

US Naval Air Station Whiting Field, Milton, Florida, 1998.

"Ah, yes . . . Missss-ter Bozung. You're back."

I had just walked in from the flight line, completely wrung out. I hoped the duty officer would just sign my grade sheet and let me leave. But I judged from his tone I probably wasn't getting off that easily.

"I just had a very interesting conversation with the Saufley RDO."

Shit. The RDO, or Runway Duty Officer, was the flight instructor who manned the shack at the approach end of the runway. Every outlying field in the Pensacola area, including Saufley Field, was manned by an RDO. He acted as an air traffic controller and safety observer to the fleet of orange and white T-34 Mentor aircraft that filled the northwest Florida skies. Calls from the RDO made to the duty officer back at base were almost never positive in nature.

Someone had typically screwed up, and the RDO wanted to ensure the student in question received a proper ass-chewing upon arrival.

"So . . . why don't *you* tell me what happened?"

Clearly, there was an ass-chewing in my future. And that didn't seem entirely fair. It was only my second solo flight. My job that day was to complete four landings at an outlying field and then proceed to one of the operating areas, where I'd practice aerobatic maneuvers for an hour or so before returning to home field. Everyone looked forward to their Precision Aerobatics, or PA solo. It was a chance to have some fun in the plane without an instructor in the back seat criticizing your every move. You got to do loops and rolls and half Cuban-eights, just like Maverick at the controls of his F-14. It was one of the highlights of the syllabus. Why did this RDO want to ruin my good time?

I retraced the events of the day. Everything had started out fine. I launched from home field, climbed to altitude, and made a quick study of my kneeboard card for the approach to Saufley Field. I'd been there a dozen times before but didn't want to leave anything to chance. All I had to do was get in the pattern, knock out my landings, and then depart. It was the rare student who found a way to screw up a solo flight. And I had no intention of being that student.

Approaching Saufley Field, I switched my radio over to button sixteen. The radios were conveniently programmed with preset channels, arranged in order of most frequent use. Button one was Ground Control. Button two was Tower. Departure Control was button three. Farther down the line, the frequency for the Saufley Field RDO was programmed as button sixteen. It was pretty handy. Rather than punch in a four-digit UHF frequency every time you wanted to switch the radio, all you had to do was click over to the preset channel.

I pushed the button on the side of the stick to key up the radio.

"Saufley RDO, Shooter Two Three Six Solo, five-mile initial, runway three two."

Translation: Hey, RDO, I'm flying a plane with the side number 6E236. I'm at the initial entry point for Saufley Field, and I'd like your permission to merge into traffic to land on runway number three two. Okay with you?

It was absolutely forbidden to enter controlled airspace without permission. The RDO had to give their consent for me to proceed inside the initial point, over the airfield for the break—the hard turn from above the runway to get into the traffic pattern—and then to descend to pattern altitude to set up for a landing. I was still sixty seconds or so outside the initial point, so the RDO and I had plenty of time to sort it all out. I maintained altitude and waited for him to call me inbound.

Ten seconds passed with no response. *That's odd*, I thought. I could see a couple of other aircraft working the pattern below me, but it didn't look that busy. Maybe the RDO just missed my call. I keyed up the mic and made the call again. Then ten more seconds . . . and nothing again. Over my left shoulder, I could see another aircraft in the distance setting up for the initial point behind me.

By then, I was only a few seconds outside the initial point, and I still didn't have permission to proceed. Worse, it appeared my radio didn't work. Losing communication, or lost comms, was an aircraft emergency and precisely what I *didn't* need only my second time driving the car without Mom or Dad. This was a scenario not covered in any portion of my training. I knew I wasn't going to descend to pattern altitude or otherwise go anywhere near the field. At the same time, I was reluctant to turn around into oncoming traffic. I called the RDO one more time, hoping the situation would just resolve itself. Again, nothing.

I didn't think I had any choice but to blow right past the initial point, so I did. And then I immediately went to work getting the hell out of there. Just as there were defined procedures to enter the airspace, so, too, were there procedures to exit. I stayed at altitude to maintain plenty of separation from the traffic working the landing pattern below. Then I turned to the prescribed heading to exit the field. I picked up the exit corridor and proceeded outbound until I was well clear. I flew on a few more miles for good measure and then did a slow, 360-degree turn to ensure there wasn't any traffic nearby.

This is just great, I thought. This little fiasco was eating into my aerobatics time. And the fact I had departed from prescribed procedures, no matter the reason, made me anxious. Good pilots made good decisions, but I lacked the experience to judge whether I had done so.

Time to troubleshoot the radio. I pulled the comms card off my kneeboard that contained frequencies for every preset channel. Then I twisted the appropriate dial on the radio console to display the frequencies that had actually been programmed. *Let's see . . . button sixteen. Did the frequencies match? Aha! They did not.* Luckily, a simple fix. I switched the radio over to manual tuning and punched in the correct frequency for Saufley Field.

Just in time to hear all hell breaking loose.

"I don't know who that joker was, but I got his side number!" It was the RDO. He was pissed.

I orbited my position several miles from the field and listened to the RDO unload on another instructor in the pattern.

"What the hell is he thinking? Some Stud thinks he can buzz my field?"

Stud was the pejorative instructor term for Student Naval Aviator.

"Well, whoever it was, that'll be his last joyride. No way is that kid staying in the flight program."

It was quite the tirade, broadcast all over northern Florida for any aircraft or nearby ham radio operator to enjoy.

And, clearly, it was all about me. If he had indeed gotten my side number, it would be easy enough to identify me as the pilot who had "buzzed" the field. And it was complete bullshit to say I'd buzzed the field, by the way. You don't buzz anything from the altitude at which

I overflew the field. I was well out of the way any other aircraft or obstruction. *Buzzed? A touch dramatic*, I thought.

But the RDO's comment about me being thrown out of the flight program had gotten my attention. If there were any truth to the statement, I at least wanted my day in court. I thought I was experiencing an aircraft emergency, for chrissakes. All things considered, I thought I'd kept a pretty level head through the whole thing and stayed safe. Maybe I could convince the RDO of that.

I sheepishly keyed up my radio. "Saufley RDO, Shooter Two Three Six solo. Uh . . . I believe the aircraft you're referring to was me. I thought I was lost comms. My presets were all screwed up. I didn't realize it until I was already inside the initial point. So then I decided to pick up the outbound course rules and clear the field. Appears I'm good to go now. Request permission to enter the pattern and knock out my landings."

The RDO took his time responding. Finally, angrily, "If you were lost comms, you should have knocked off the approach and turned around. You've got no business coming anywhere near this field without my permission. Get down here, get your landings done, and get back to base."

"Yes, sir. Two Three Six inbound."

I knew fessing up was the right thing to do. But my nerves were shot. I entered the break, flew a mediocre downwind—that portion of the traffic pattern opposite the direction of landing—and then put together four of the shittiest landings I'd ever done. In my haste to get it all over with, I was cutting power too soon at the approach end of the field and touching down in front of the RDO shack, not beyond it as the rules required.

"Uh, Two Three Six, you mind landing farther down the runway? I'd rather not die today. Thanks." The RDO was not impressed.

I finished my landings and headed back to home field. The duty officer was expecting me. I had no time for aerobatics. Frankly, I really wasn't in the mood for any yankin' and bankin' anyway. At that point, all I wanted to do was live to fight another day. *Let's get this over with,*

I told myself. *Let's just get it over with.* All those years at the Academy sweating calculus, chemistry, physics, electrical engineering, and countless other mind-numbing technical courses just to get a seat in that cockpit could have been for naught. And it would all be thanks to my goddamned radio. The very thought was nauseating.

I told the duty officer my story. Yes, I had proceeded inside the initial point, but I had remained safely at altitude and followed proper exit procedures. And I didn't want to break off my approach, because I didn't want to turn into the traffic behind me. Overflying the field without permission from the RDO seemed the least bad of all available options.

The lieutenant wasn't buying it. "The *correct* action would have been to immediately break off the approach! So what if there was someone behind you? Are you telling me you couldn't have turned around without smacking into him? You were VFR!"

Visual Flight Rules, or VFR, meant the principle of *see and avoid* applied. If you see another aircraft, make the necessary maneuvers to avoid it. It was one of the most basic, common-sense rules of flight.

I stood there with my eyes forward and heels locked. The duty officer's voice rose as he gathered momentum.

"I should send you to see the skipper right now. You never, ever bust anyone's airspace without permission. That's how you get a flight violation. Or killed."

"Yes, sir." I'd said my piece. No point in arguing now.

"Give me your grade sheet."

I handed it over. *This ought to be it*, I thought.

The lieutenant picked up a pen and ran it down the list of graded items on the sheet. Every evolution, from preflight brief to final shutdown, was subject to evaluation. Students received marks ranging from unsatisfactory to above average. An exceptionally good flight, or *hop*, could earn a student average marks in most areas, with above-average scores on two items, for a net score of *two-above*. An exceptionally bad hop, which earned a student average scores on most items and a below-average grade in two areas, was known as a *two-below*. The Chuck Yeagers of the world racked up numerous two-above hops. Guys like me, who fell right in the meaty part of the bell curve, posted mostly average scores, with the occasional one or two-above hop. And those students who collected too many two-belows, or worse, typically washed out of the flight training program and went on to drive ships or serve in some other capacity.

There was obviously less an instructor could observe on a solo flight, so there were fewer items on this grade sheet. But the two most important items remained—*procedures* and *headwork*. These were the two items on which you *never* wanted to score below average. Procedures was a general assessment of whether you performed maneuvers by the book. Headwork evaluated your situational awareness and decision-making capability. Were you thinking *ahead of the plane* or *hopelessly behind*? In other words, were you able to rapidly and accurately assess your situation, determine the appropriate course of action based upon that assessment, and then proceed upon that course without undue hesitation or delay? To act always in accordance with procedures and exhibit strong headwork was to be a fundamentally sound pilot.

Should you be found wanting in either area, the odds of your earning your wings and flying off of ships for a living were incredibly low.

The lieutenant looked up from the sheet and directly at me. My eyes remained locked straight ahead. After a moment's contemplation, he returned to the grade sheet and rendered his verdict.

"One-below for headwork."

What? One below for headwork? On a solo? My mind raced. I'd never heard of such a thing. No one ever got a below-average on a solo. I didn't think it was even possible.

My jaw clenched. *The injustice!* I considered arguing but thought better of it. That would only make the situation worse. The lieutenant handed me my grade sheet and told me to leave.

Word of my notoriety quickly spread among the other students. "That's the guy who got a one-below on his PA solo. Can you believe it?" It was embarrassing. My buddies were merciless. They were convinced I was the first student in the history of Naval aviation to distinguish himself in such a fashion. They encouraged me to frame my grade sheet. Dumbasses.

Several months later, I was at the controls of a TH-57 Jet Ranger helicopter. A buddy of mine, also a student, sat next to me as copilot. No instructor was in the aircraft. We were returning to home field from one of the operating areas. I switched up the tower frequency, which was clobbered with non-stop chatter. It was a busy day.

I waited for an opening, then quickly checked in with the controller.

"Tower, Factoryhand Five Five, two-mile initial, full stop, runway three-two."

"Standby," he said. "Expect clearance one mike."

We were still outside the tower's airspace and were advised to expect permission to enter in one minute, or *mike*. A few seconds later, he came back over the radio and cleared another aircraft in. When that aircraft did not immediately respond, he repeated the call. Again, no response. He called a third time, clearly agitated. No response.

"You think he's talking to us?" I asked my buddy. "Did he screw up our callsign?"

We were inside two miles of the field's airspace and still hadn't been cleared in. "I've seen this movie before," I told my buddy. "If we don't get cleared in the next sixty seconds, we're turning around." No *way* did I intend to lock my heels in front of another pissed-off duty officer. I'd learned my lesson.

Just then, another aircraft checked in. The controller told it to standby. Again, he tried to clear in the other aircraft.

Finally, I called the tower. "Understand you're calling Factoryhand Five *Five*?" He'd been saying Five *Four*.

That did the trick. Yes, the controller had confused our callsign. He cleared us in, and we landed without incident.

Back at the duty office, the lieutenant on duty signed our grade sheets.

"Anything interesting happen out there?"

Not a thing, sir. Not a thing.

LESSONS LEARNED

1. Ass-chewings can be very useful. They allow the chew-er to set and maintain important organizational standards. And they provide the chew-ee real-time, corrective feedback to avoid potential calamity. Upperclassmen chewed my ass at the Naval Academy. Flight instructors chewed my ass in Pensacola. Bosses have chewed my ass. My wife routinely chews my ass. And customers seem to especially enjoy chewing my ass. Often, it's for good reason.

2. But not all ass-chewings are created equal. Some are delivered by those who possess the proper positional authority but lack the moral authority. Asshole bosses typically fall into this category. Such ass-chewings must simply be endured. Other ass-chewings are delivered by those who may lack positional authority but possess ample moral authority. Those should be taken to heart.

    I once sent my five-year-old daughter to her room for some minor, little-kid infraction. Ten minutes later, when I went to her room to release her from time-out, I found taped to her door a note that read, "I love you daddy. Plez frgme."

    The message was clear and damning. "Please forgive me. I'm just a little kid. You over-reacted, and it hurt my feelings. But I still love you."

    That was easily the most elegant and complete ass-chewing I'd ever received. And it will both shame and inspire me for the remainder of my days.

3. The best response to an ass-chewing is almost always to take it, get over it, and learn your lesson. Carry on!

Get on Centerline

"You have a lot going for you, Dan, but . . ."

Kaneohe Bay, Hawaii, 2000.

I survived the remainder of flight training without further incident. And when it came time to graduate and make my list of desired duty stations, one location stood above all others on my dream sheet: Hawaii. The Navy generously granted me my first choice and I was shipped off to join a squadron in paradise as a newly minted SH-60B Seahawk helicopter pilot.

Weeks later, shortly after taking off for my first Oahu familiarization flight, I found myself gawking at a sprawling compound outside Waimanalo as it passed down the right side of the aircraft.

"Look familiar?" my new squadron mate asked.

Vaguely, I thought.

Then it hit me.

"Wait a minute. Is that the Robin Masters estate?"

"That's right!"

Yes, it was the same house used to film *Magnum, PI* episodes in the 1980s.

Holy shit! I could be Thomas Magnum right now!

The small-town Michigan kid in me could hardly believe the luck. I mean, I was looking at *the* Robin's Nest. It was surreal. *So this is what flying in Hawaii's all about? Right on!* The *Magnum, PI* theme song started running through my head. "Da-da-da-DUH!" *Now, where's that red Ferrari?*

Unfortunately, the feeling was short-lived. Reality smacked me in the face a short time later when I learned I was scheduled to fly the next day with the CO, the squadron's commanding officer.

I wanted to fly with the CO like I wanted a flaming case of hemorrhoids. As a helicopter second pilot, or H2P, every minute of every flight was subject to both formal and informal evaluation. Everything was a graded evolution. That presented no fewer than a thousand opportunities for me to screw something up and look like an idiot in the eyes of our squadron's most experienced and highly decorated pilots. Christ! The *Old Man* had spent his earliest days in the cockpit slaloming through Persian Gulf oil fields on black-ass nights during Operation Praying Mantis—our brief scuffle with Iran during the Tanker War of the late-1980s. He'd been awarded an Air Medal with Combat *V* for Valor during Desert Storm. He'd been shot at. He'd flown in a scene in *The Hunt for Red October*. He was built like a linebacker and had a voice that boomed deeper and about 100 decibels louder than anyone else's. He loved Budweiser and insisted you should, too. He made it abundantly clear that his alma mater, Notre Dame, was the only respectable school in the country and that yours was shit. He was the life of the party, with a quick, punishing wit. A kind word from the skipper left you euphoric; a sharp word stung for weeks.

I made it through the flight brief, pre-flight inspection, and start-up checklist as well as could be expected. It was an absolutely perfect, crystal-clear, South Pacific morning, with the trade winds blowing steadily from the northwest and a temperature just shy of eighty degrees. The plan was to depart Kaneohe and follow Oahu's northern coast before turning south to the center of the island and Wheeler Army Airfield for some pattern work.

Shortly after I lifted off the pad at the northwest corner of the field and made a climbing right turn over Kaneohe Bay for departure, the skipper asked, "So . . . let's say you had a single-engine failure right now. What would you do?"

"Well, sir," I explained, "given that we're not even at five hundred feet, I'd get the nose pointed into the wind and set up for a ditch." That was the procedure called for in the manual, and I wasn't aware of any better or different solution to that problem.

"You'd do what?" he asked in near-disgust. "You'd put a perfectly good aircraft with *one* operating engine in the water when you have an entire runway not even a thousand yards away? You sure about that?"

Shit. I quickly realized he'd said *single* engine failure, not *dual.* That, of course, called for an entirely different procedure, one that most definitely did not end in ditching. I meekly explained to the skipper that I'd misheard him and recited the proper emergency procedure for a single-engine failure. *This is off to a great start,* I thought.

The mood lightened somewhat on the way to Wheeler. It's hard not to be happy when you're booming down the Hawaiian coastline with mountains and pineapple fields on one side of the aircraft and rich, azure-blue ocean on the other.

I called up the tower at Wheeler and received permission to enter the pattern. I'd done all the flying to that point, and the skipper gave no indication he intended to grab the controls. I descended to pattern altitude, called for the landing checklist, and started maneuvering the aircraft to maintain the runway numbers in the bottom half of the windshield, exactly as I'd been taught in flight training. Conditions were ideal: light winds right down the center of the runway, little-to-no traffic in the pattern, and a friendly, accommodating controller in the tower.

I was feeling a hell of a lot better than I had upon leaving Kaneohe. The controls felt good in my hands, and I was executing maneuvers with confidence. It appeared I'd turned things around.

About a half mile from touchdown, the skipper abruptly interrupted my self-congratulating with the words all H2Ps dread.

"I have the controls."

"Roger, you have the controls," I immediately replied.

He added power, began climbing back to pattern altitude, and informed the tower, "Easyrider Six Three's going around."

Not good. I quickly scanned my memory of the previous five minutes for any indiscretion, no matter how small. Nothing. I couldn't think of a single thing I'd done wrong. In the meantime, the skipper had set up for an extended downwind and slowed the aircraft to ninety knots. Something was clearly on his mind.

After a long, uncomfortable silence, he asked, "Do you know why I took the controls?"

"No, sir."

"Because you weren't on centerline."

The centerline was the imaginary line that extended from the middle of the runway up and through the airspace at the approach end.

Not on centerline? So what? I was *close* to centerline, maybe a degree or two off, tops, but good enough for government work, as the saying goes. It was an absolutely perfect day, with an unlimited ceiling and visibility, and I clearly had the runway made. Barring catastrophic mechanical failure, there was no way I was going to screw up that landing. And it was a helicopter, for chrissakes. If there was even the remotest chance of missing the runway, I could literally stop in midair and fly backwards, if necessary, to make it back. *Not on centerline? Who gives a shit?*

Then, in a calm, fatherly, but nonetheless serious tone, the skipper explained why being exactly on centerline was so important.

First, there were practical reasons. While that day offered ideal flying conditions, Navy pilots always had to prepare themselves to operate in the absolute worst. Every approach should be flown as though they were in the middle of the ocean, well out of range of land, on a black-ass night with no visible horizon, almost out of gas, with a copilot incapacitated by vertigo, and aiming for a flight deck tossed by heavy seas and gyrating like the back of a mechanical bull. *That* was the environment in which Naval aviators earned their pay.

"We're *military* pilots," he explained, "not goddamn tour operators."

A single degree off centerline under less than ideal conditions could mean the difference between finding the ship and making a safe landing and flaming out one's fuel-starved engines and going swimming. It came down to discipline and the cultivation of correct habits. Always, always be prepared for the worst.

Second, on a more philosophical note, we were professionals, he explained. "And professionals accept *nothing less than perfection.*"

Sure, there was plenty about being in the Navy every pilot in the squadron took less than seriously, the skipper included. And when it was time to crack open a beer, he invariably led the charge. But when it came to the cockpit, and the demands of safely operating aircraft from warships plying some of the most dangerous waters in the world, he was deadly serious. And he expected every aviator in his charge to be the same.

"You have a lot going for you, Dan. But it's obvious you haven't made up your mind whether you want to be a professional."

Was the skipper suggesting I wasn't a professional? *The nerve! I'm Dan Bozung. I've been good at everything I've ever done. My mom told me so.*

No one had ever challenged me that way. And he was exactly right to do so. My standards were set unacceptably low. I wore the Wings of Gold, but I wasn't a professional.

Sure enough, only a few months later, I found myself in exactly the sort of worst-case scenario the skipper had described. I was flying with Woody, a seasoned aircraft commander, about 100 miles off the coast of San Diego. It was late afternoon, and we were scheduled to land on the ship just before sunset. We'd been out searching for an "enemy" submarine as part of an exercise, with zero luck. Our search had revealed no trace of any submarine. We thought we'd found it at one point, but realized it was a whale. Finding a sub that doesn't want to be found can be very tedious, frustrating work.

We turned toward the ship, which was steaming about twenty-five miles to our east. The situation at that point was pretty unremarkable: calm seas, scattered clouds, and a clear horizon. I was sitting in the left seat, where all the aircraft's tactical controls and displays were situated. Woody, over in the right seat, thought it would be good practice for me to man the left seat and lead the search for the sub, no matter how unfruitful the effort. He was probably right, although I much preferred flying from the right seat to button-pushing from the left.

We closed to within fifteen miles of the ship. Suddenly, this big, gray, opaque wall of cloud appeared out of nowhere and totally obscured the ocean in front of us. Woody quickly locked his eyes on the aircraft attitude indicator, banked into a tight turn, and reversed course to maintain a visual horizon. No way did we want to fly blindly through that stuff. Woody then climbed a few thousand feet to get above the clouds and did a slow turn back in the direction of the ship to get the full picture of what we were up against. Beneath us was spread a solid blanket of clouds stretching as far as we could see to the north and east, from the ocean's surface up to about a thousand feet. Somewhere in that mess, the ship awaited us with a clear flight deck and hot cheeseburgers.

"No worries," said Woody. "Marine layer. Blows in out of nowhere. Typical this time of year. We'll just hang out here and have the ship drive to us."

That made perfect sense. Woody called up the ship, explained the situation, and soon it was making way in our direction. He then slowed the aircraft to conserve fuel and started flying a lazy, figure eight pattern to maintain our position. Textbook.

After a few minutes, the Landing Signals Officer, or LSO, one of our fellow pilots aboard the ship, called us.

"How's it look up there?"

"Fine," Woody answered. "How's it look down there?"

"Terrible. Can't see your hand in front of your face. Solid goo. Visibility about a tenth of a mile, maybe less."

All the more reason for the ship to come to us. We knocked out our landing checklist and waited for our *green deck* to land. As we did, the marine layer seemed to morph and expand in all directions. Woody kept pushing farther to the west to avoid it. But, eventually, he couldn't. It was everywhere. The entire ocean beneath us was completely socked in. It was getting dark. And, of course, we were getting low on fuel.

It was by no means an emergency, but we definitely did not have the gas to make it back to the beach. We'd have enough for a few passes at the ship, if needed, before landing with the minimal amount allowed. As the skipper would say, Woody and I would be earning our paychecks that night.

"Easyrider Six Two, you have a green deck for one and one." The LSO was waving us in for one approach and one landing.

I was a little anxious, but not too concerned. This may have been my first experience landing in such conditions, but not Woody's. Not even close. By all standards of Naval aviation, he was a professional. He was a graduate of the Navy's prestigious Test Pilot School. Woody knew the extreme edge of the Sikorsky SH-60B Seahawk operating envelope more intimately than almost any other pilot in the Navy. He had a few thousand flight hours under his belt and was far and away one of the most coolheaded, easygoing pilots in the ready room. I knew he wasn't anxious. If anything, he was having fun.

Woody set up for the approach while I buckled down to do some serious copiloting. A good copilot enhanced a pilot's situational awareness by providing them the right cues, at the right time, without distracting them with too much information. It was my job to back Woody up on every aircraft operating parameter: altitude, airspeed, heading, rate of closure, glideslope, and position relative to the ship. Like anything, it required both skill and finesse to be a good copilot, which could only be gained through experience.

As I scanned the instruments, I could see Woody had us *exactly* on centerline, *exactly* on airspeed, and *exactly* on glideslope. The standard approach took us down to two hundred feet and a half-mile behind the ship, at which point the flight deck should be in view. But on this go-around, it wasn't. Woody pressed-in to a quarter mile, but still no flight deck. We couldn't see the ship at all. Not wanting to smack into the back of the hangar, Woody broke off the approach and turned outbound to set up for another pass. We climbed back to altitude and rebriefed the approach. We'd done everything right but couldn't get a visual.

"Hey, it happens," Woody said.

The LSO called. "Yeah, I could hear you, but I couldn't see anything. It's getting pretty thick down here."

Back on the approach, Woody flew with the same, exacting precision. Yet it yielded the same result: no ship.

We turned outbound once again to set up for our third approach. As we did, we reviewed our options. We didn't have enough gas to go searching for a clear patch of ocean. We'd have to land right where we were. Maybe we could fly the next approach below minimum altitude and just creep the aircraft slowly forward until the ship came within sight. That wasn't ideal, because such a maneuver could quickly induce vertigo, or the leans, a dangerous, disorienting condition made even more so at low altitude.

As a last resort, we could call for a smoke light approach, whereby someone on the ship would throw flares in the water at regular intervals, giving us a glowing trail of breadcrumbs to follow all the way to the stern. Woody had never done one, but he'd heard of cases in which it had worked.

We decided we had enough gas for one more, normal approach. If that didn't work, we'd try creeping it in. And we called the ship and told them to get the flares ready, just in case.

Once again, Woody put us exactly on profile and flew another textbook approach. We pushed to within a quarter mile, slowed to a near-hover, and decided to keep going. Woody remained preternaturally calm. He hadn't even broken a sweat. He maintained an alert, yet comfortable posture and smoothly made micro-corrections on the stick. It was beautiful.

I wish I could have said the same for myself. Sweat was dripping into my eyes, and I leaned forward in my seat, my face only inches from the instruments. Somewhere below and in front of us was a ship, with all sorts of masts and antennas to get tangled in. And well inside a quarter mile, we still couldn't see the damn thing. I watched the Distance Measuring Equipment, or DME, tick down to two tenths of a mile . . . then one tenth.

Then, a moment later, as I was about to call for a wave-off, the outlines of a ship appeared through the chin bubble beneath our feet.

We both saw it at the same time. *Shit!* We'd overshot the flight deck and were directly over the main mast, just aft of the bridge. Woody instinctively pulled power, but then caught himself. If we climbed, we'd end up back in the goo. But if we descended, we risked colliding with the mast. So, Woody just held position and stabilized the aircraft in a perfect hover.

"I'm gonna hold it here and let the ship drive out from underneath us."

"Uh . . . okay . . ."

Sure enough, the ship moved out from underneath us, and the flight deck came within view. It was easy from there. Woody set us in a low hover exactly on the lineup lines and planted a perfect landing. It was one of the most amazing feats of airmanship I'd ever witnessed.

As the flight deck crew set the chocks and chains on the landing gear, I glanced at the fuel gauge. We'd landed with almost precisely 600 pounds, the minimally prescribed amount of fuel. I pointed it out to Woody, who responded, "Of course."

We sat there for a while without saying anything. I realized I'd sweated through the entire back side of my flight suit. Woody just stared ahead, watching the activities on the flight deck as we prepared to shut down.

Eventually, he turned in my direction and uttered, in true, understated, Woody fashion, "Damn. That was hard."

LESSONS LEARNED

1. It's obvious to everyone when you're not making your best effort. At a minimum, it erodes your credibility. At worst, it gets someone killed. And if you're in a leadership position, it causes your subordinates to doubt you, doubt themselves, and doubt the purpose of whatever endeavor you're leading. People instinctively respond to a leader's subtlest cues. And if those cues suggest the leader is half-assing it, others will do the same.

2. If you can't be a professional at whatever you're doing, find something else. You risk significant harm to your effectiveness and reputation if you persist in a role in which you're either unable or unwilling to be your very best. It causes people to experience you negatively and closes doors to future opportunities. Don't allow that to happen. Make a change, soon.

3. It's inspiring to observe a professional at work. So get your ass on centerline! Strive to be that professional.

Ashtray

Lord, please do *not* let me embarrass my boss

Atlantic City, New Jersey, 2003.

The ash on my cigar had grown to about three-and-a-half inches. With every second that ticked by, I pushed my luck a little further. Without an ashtray, trash can, potted plant, or gutter anywhere within reach, I risked sending a gray, sooty mess to the pristine, off-white carpet underfoot—a total rookie move.

I considered my options. I was standing in the corner of a swanky, upstairs bar in an Atlantic City casino. Could I discreetly slip the ash into my pocket? Negative. I didn't have one. I was dressed in my Navy Dinner Dress Whites, a cocktail waiter-looking uniform with a short white jacket, cummerbund, and pocketless pants. It was hardly practical attire for the crisis at hand. Could I steal an ashtray from a nearby table? Not happening. Around those tables sat half of all the active duty four-star generals in the Marine Corps. Being the only Navy lieutenant in the room, I wasn't about to interrupt those conversations. My job was to be neither seen nor heard. What if I simply held the ash in my hand? That would be fine until I was presented to one of those four-stars. "Sorry, General. I must decline a handshake. You see, funny thing, I have this handful of cigar ash . . ." When I'd accepted that cigar, I really hadn't thought the whole thing through.

And what about my boss? *Lord, please do* not *let me embarrass my boss*, I thought. Upon completion of my squadron tour in Hawaii, I had been nominated to serve as the executive assistant to the US Naval Academy's first Marine Corps Commandant of Midshipmen. It was a terrific honor just to have been selected, let alone occupy a position of special trust with one of the military's most accomplished, up-and-coming senior officers. And so what if he was a Marine?

This was the colonel's coming-out party, of sorts. He had recently been selected for promotion to brigadier general. Ever since, invitations to exclusive, general officers-only events had poured in. This was the most star-studded to date. As his executive assistant, I had been granted access behind the velvet rope. The colonel had very generously afforded me glimpses of such events, because he trusted me and treated me like a varsity player. I, in turn, endeavored to earn that trust every day by not making junior varsity mistakes like throwing cigar ash around the carpeted floors of upscale bars full of officers wearing multiple stars on their shoulders. It was a pretty simple pact.

The colonel stood twenty feet away with this his back turned toward me. He was chatting with General "Spider" Nyland, the assistant commandant of the Marine Corps, oblivious to my growing crisis. Or so I thought. About the time I considered eating the cigar ash, I watched the colonel, mid-sentence, thrust his arm into the middle of one of the tables occupied by generals, deftly retrieve an ashtray, offer a quick, "Excuse me, General," to Spider Nyland, take five steps in my direction, hand me the ashtray, and then casually resume his conversation. It all happened in about five seconds. Dumbfounded, I relieved my cigar of the burden of its perilously long ash. Crisis averted.

I have no idea how the colonel, surrounded by a galaxy of stars, could have been so attuned to the anxieties of his young lieutenant. Were you to ask him about it today, I'm sure he would have no recollection of giving me that ashtray. That's just who he is. Nevertheless, to me, it was a profound moment of humility and generosity that exemplified the very finest of servant leadership. I will never forget it.

LESSONS LEARNED

1. Whether employees go the extra mile has a lot to do with the extent to which they feel valued by their boss. And it takes remarkably little. Simple, genuine acts of courtesy are often all that is required to keep team members productive and engaged. Don't think for a second that a brief "thank you" or "nicely done" is a waste of time. Show your people you value them, and they will run through walls for you.

2. You won't always know what impact you have on people. But, if you routinely treat everyone you encounter with dignity and respect, the odds are strongly in favor of you positively influencing the lives of many, many people.

3. Never be too busy, too tired, too distracted, or in too much of a hurry to appreciate your people.

Own It!

"As I said, Senator, I am not an accountant."

Harvard Business School, 2005.

A plebe is taught the Five Basic Responses within the first ninety seconds of his or her arrival at the Naval Academy. From that point forward, the only acceptable answers to any question posed, short of fully and truthfully answering it, are:

1. Yes, sir.
2. No, sir.
3. I'll find out, sir.
4. No excuse, sir.
5. Aye, aye, sir.

The latter, surviving from the days of sail, translates as: "I understand the order you've given, and I will carry it out smartly."

Absent from the list of Five Basic Responses are statements like: "I don't know," "Well, it depends," and "You'd have to ask (some other person)." Nope, that shit doesn't fly. Such statements evidence a lack of ownership. They enable the respondent to evade responsibility for those things for which he or she should rightly be held accountable. They suggest a lack of moral courage, which is total anathema to a military officer. As a nation, we've entrusted our military leaders to operate independently in far-off places with the lives of our sons and daughters in their hands. Only persons of the highest integrity can be so entrusted, and the way they take ownership of issues through forthright answers to hard questions says a lot about the strength of their character.

It was with the Five Basic Responses in mind that I grew nauseated as I listened to Jeffrey Skilling in February of 2002. Skilling, Enron's former CEO and a Harvard Business School graduate, appeared before the Senate Commerce, Science, and Transportation Committee. I had left the active duty Navy only months before to seize the unexpected opportunity to attend Harvard, although I remained affiliated with the service through the Navy Reserve. My classmates and I were watching a recording of Skilling's appearance in our first-year finance class. The question on the table was, how was Enron's spectacular collapse allowed to happen?

I thought it had everything to do with Skilling's complete lack of accountability. Many of the Senators seemed to believe the same.

Jean Carnahan of Missouri: "Mr. Skilling, if you plan to tell this committee that you did not understand Enron's true financial condition, then you will need to explain why you failed to understand things that any diligent CEO would have understood. And if you insist that you were unaware of the company's financial condition, then I hope that you are prepared to explain why you portrayed yourself as someone who did."

Later, John McCain of Arizona had the following exchange with Skilling regarding his knowledge of *raptor* transactions, highly technical financial instruments allegedly intended to paper-over Enron's losses.

Skilling: "When Ms. Watkins (a former Enron accountant and whistleblower) talks about a restructuring or the fact that, you know, what I knew or didn't know, my only recollection of the restructuring of the raptors is that I was told that they were restructuring the raptors. I asked if the accountants had signed off on it, if it looked okay, and I was told that it was, and went along with it."

McCain: "Was it your responsibility to know?"

Skilling: "Sorry?"

McCain: "Was it your responsibility to know?"

Skilling: "As I said, Senator, I am not an accountant. These are highly, highly—I think if you will look in the October minutes at the structure of raptor, this is—this is a complex, complex structure. And it took, I think, quite some time for Arthur Andersen, as I recall, this was even taken to Arthur Andersen's technical group in Chicago because it was so technical, and they signed off and said that they thought this was the appropriate accounting treatment."

Blah, blah, blah . . .

Senator John McCain, US Naval Academy Class of 1958, former Naval aviator and prisoner of war, *the maverick*, he got it. He knew all about accountability. And Skilling, through his exchange with McCain, made it perfectly clear he intended not to accept a single ounce of it. It was disgusting.

In the discussion that followed the hearing, I could hardly contain myself. I felt compelled to share my disgust with the entire class. As one of the few military guys in the school, it was my duty to mount my white horse and give all the Wall Street alums in the room a lesson on what integrity in a leader *really* meant. Where I came from, the commanding officer owned *everything* that took place on his watch. No explaining. No deflecting. No well-the-accountants-told-me bullshit. Own it!

Upon making comments to that effect, a classmate, with a look of mild amusement on her face, observed, "you know, Dan, the difference between your world and Skilling's is that you get celebrated for 'owning it,' while Skilling gets to go to jail."

Wait. What?

Skilling did indeed go to jail. He was indicted on thirty-five counts, found guilty on nineteen, and was sentenced to twenty-four years, of which he ultimately served twelve.

My classmate's comment stopped me cold. As a graduate student recently released from active duty, I didn't know jack shit about life in the private sector. I only knew the cozy comfort of Mother Navy's womb. Could it be that accountability was so deeply ingrained in the military culture, because, in part, prison was seldom the consequence for those commanders who *owned it*?

I was reminded of an incident from the same era involving the *Ehime Maru*, a Japanese fishing training vessel sunk by a Navy submarine just south of Oahu.

Just before 1:45 p.m. on February 9, 2001, the submarine, *USS Greeneville*, then submerged, executed an emergency ballast blow that sent it shooting to the surface, directly underneath the *Ehime Maru*. Nine Japanese aboard were killed in the ensuing collision: four students, two teachers, and three crew members.

Commander Scott Waddle, *Greeneville's* commanding officer, was immediately relieved of command. The Navy convened a court of inquiry to investigate the incident, whose members ultimately recommended non-judicial punishment for Waddle in lieu of courts-martial due to a lack of criminal intent. While Waddle was publicly criticized for his perceived lack of remorse in the immediate aftermath of the incident, he took full responsibility for it during the inquiry. He received no jail time, but was instead issued a formal reprimand and was made to forfeit some amount of pay. By year's end, he was allowed to formally retire from the Navy, with full pay and benefits intact. Suffice it to say the Japanese were *not* pleased with this outcome.

How is it that accountability looked so different in these two cases? Skilling destroyed billions of dollars in value and laid waste to thousands of people's livelihoods. He was locked up as a result. Waddle was responsible for the deaths of nine innocent Japanese. He remained free, drew a generous government pension, and retained the privilege to buy tax-free liquor at any package store on any US military base in the world for the rest of his life.

"Wait just a damn minute," some may say. The cases of Skilling and Waddle hardly make for a fair comparison. One willfully engaged in, or at least turned a blind eye to, criminal activity, while the other was simply an unfortunate bystander to a terrible accident. It is both unreasonable and inappropriate to expect similar consequences for the derelictions of both leaders.

Maybe. But I do think these incidents illustrate quite nicely the wide disparity that exists between the military and civilian cultures of accountability.

Waddle's world was very different from Skilling's. The military community enjoys a wide social and financial safety net that the civilian population does not. An average performer in the military who keeps their nose clean is all but guaranteed a steady paycheck, housing allowances, and top-quality medical care for at least twenty years, maybe longer. And upon retiring after those twenty years, many of those benefits continue until death, with some extending until the spouse's death.

There are exceptions, of course. Every now and then, the military goes through a reduction in force and throws a certain percentage of its under-performing population out on the street. And the services certainly have their fair share of criminals behind bars in places like Leavenworth. Nonetheless, I think it's fair to say that members of our military enjoy both job security and a reasonably high quality of life. They may want for some things, but they need for very little.

Once upon a time, the same could be said of the civilian workforce. Large corporations offered *employment for life*, and it wasn't unusual for working men and women to have only one employer for their entire careers. Generous, defined-benefit pensions, earned at a reasonably young age, provided both financial security and a comfortable standard of living. Those were the days our parents and grandparents enjoyed. And they're long, long gone.

Security, social and financial, largely determines one's risk tolerance. And there are times when forthrightness carries risk.

Honesty might not always be the best policy, it turns out, if one wants to avoid prison time and preserve one's livelihood. That was a totally foreign concept to me, having worn the uniform since age seventeen. Honesty was the *only* policy, as far as I was concerned. And, to be clear, it still is.

However, I am much, much more guarded than I ever was while on active duty. I was once a true believer in the kind of *Radical Candor* Kim Scott advocated in her terrific book of that title and prided myself on being the consummate straight shooter. But while my integrity remains fully intact, I have come to appreciate as a civilian that radical candor and a predilection to assume responsibility do indeed carry risk. I am far less the straight shooter as a result.

And why? When someone gets *fired* in the military, they are typically reassigned to a less desirable position. They remain on the payroll, and, provided whatever got them reassigned wasn't too egregious, have a reasonable shot at continuing their military career, even promoting.

By contrast, when civilians get fired, their asses are *terminated*, as in, pack-up-your-shit-and-security-will-escort-you-out. Most companies offer some form of severance, but that only takes a person so far, particularly in a bad economy. Eventually, savings dry up, IRAs get cashed out, and college funds get emptied. And in addition to the financial strain, there's the anxiety and self-loathing they get to enjoy while prostituting themselves to the job market and growing increasingly desperate for someone, anyone, to make an offer. Yeah, it's a real treat. And if that person is the sole breadwinner of a family with bodies to clothe and mouths to feed, the misery of the experience is increased fiftyfold.

I've never been fired in the military, but I have been *fired* in the private sector. And it's an experience to which I would go terrific lengths not to repeat.

That may well include forsaking the Five Basic Responses.

LESSONS LEARNED

1. The naïve idealist I was upon leaving active duty couldn't imagine the possibility of a leader not taking full responsibility for their own conduct and that of their organization. I now understand not every culture rewards those who *own it*.

    There's a clear downside to taking responsibility. But that doesn't mean you shouldn't. Yes, it carries risk. But leaders who foster strong cultures of accountability build organizations that stand the test of time.

2. It's easier to *own it* when you're inspired to serve a cause greater than yourself. The military readily provides such inspiration. The preservation of the American way of life through our national defense can be heady stuff.

    I've found that civilians are far less inspired. For some, the only cause worth serving is one's own. And that's perfectly fine. Maybe you won't get a parade thrown in your honor, but you can still provide a useful service.

    Some of the best salespeople I know don't give a shit about their companies or the purposes they supposedly serve. But they know how to move product and make money. That's good for them and their companies.

3. I used to wonder why my business school classmates were so amused when I would say exactly what I was thinking in class. "Such honesty, such candor, so . . . refreshing," they'd say.

    And stupid, it turns out, in certain settings. Forthrightness was expected, even required, in the military. The culture supported it. But not all cultures do.

    I once served up a dose of candor to a civilian colleague and promptly landed myself in hot water with Human Resources. That was dumb. I should have known better.

The Pursuit of Passion

"I think it's time to end the experiment."

Watertown, Massachusetts, 2006.

I took an immediate wrong turn out of business school when I foolishly decided to pursue my passion.

It started during the summer between the Required and Elective Curricula, or RC and EC year. Most of my classmates were either sitting in Manhattan skyscrapers as summer associates for the world's most prestigious investment banks or power lunching with the clients of leading consulting firms. Not me. I was digging a ditch. Specifically, I was digging the footing for the main stairway of a new addition to an eighteenth-century farmhouse. I was part of a three-man crew working for one of the finest residential construction companies in Cambridge, Massachusetts. Despite being in decent shape, my body hadn't yet fully adjusted to the pounding of continuous, daylong, manual labor. My back hurt and my work gloves had failed to prevent both my palms from blistering. It was beautiful.

This was where my passion had apparently led me. All the career coaches in the MBA career services office beat the same, steady drumbeat: to discover your true career is to follow your passion. "Let your passion guide you," they'd said.

Okay. I could grasp the concept. But what, in practical terms, did that mean? And what if you weren't even sure you were passionate about anything? Then what?

"Well," they'd say, "just think about those activities in which you become so fully engrossed that you lose all track of time. Therein you will find your passion."

Great. For me, those activities included watching *Seinfeld* reruns, napping, and smoking expensive cigars. They all met career services' lose-all-track-of-time criteria, but I struggled to discern any viable career opportunities in any of those activities. So what then?

I had become a huge fan of the PBS show *The New Yankee Workshop*. The host, Master Carpenter Norm Abram, would find these incredible pieces of rare, centuries-old furniture in antique shops throughout New England and then take them back to his wood shop to produce exact replicas. Every episode would follow Norm, step-by-step, through this process while he provided continuous commentary in his thick, Massachusetts accent ("And remem-bah, we'll want to finish this cor-nah with a nice, shahp chisel"). No Saturday morning was complete without Norm, and it thrilled me to be living in the same state in which he'd risen to soaring heights of public television fame.

As the first year of business school wound to a close and my classmates hit the exits for their summer banking and consulting gigs, I thought of Norm. With a router spinning in his hands, sporting that trademark flannel shirt, he was truly in the zone. Here was a guy who spent absolutely *zero* time trying to discern his passion, while producing objects of incredible beauty and real, lasting value. He had an air of contentment any of the career coaches would have admired. This guy had figured it out. I wanted to be like Norm. Dammit, I wanted to build something!

Of course, the only problem was I had absolutely no mechanical ability whatsoever. I could barely hammer a nail straight, let alone produce practical objects of enduring beauty using power tools. Nonetheless, I had an entire summer in front of me to do whatever I pleased. Sure, conventional business school wisdom suggested I follow the herd to Wall Street, but I had absolutely no interest in doing that. I had the rest of my life to drive a desk in the corporate world. It might be decades before I'd have another opportunity to spend any significant time learning to build something.

I got online and searched out construction firms in Cambridge, Massachusetts. My plan was to compile a list of such firms, send introductory letters to each, and then follow up the letters with phone calls. My letter was short and to the point. I explained I was a transitioning veteran with a desire to learn construction and that I sought a full-time summer position to explore whether the industry might be a fit. I absolutely did *not* mention I was a Harvard student. This was a situation, I reasoned, in which a lot of pedigree probably wouldn't do me much good. In fact, it might even hurt my chances of landing a position.

About a week after I sent out my letters, I got a call from the owner of one of the firms. He said he was always interested in helping veterans and invited me to an interview. The following Tuesday, I jumped on my bike and pedaled across Cambridge to his office to sell him on my summer internship idea. It didn't take much selling. Summer was a busy time in the construction business, and the owner was looking for people to fill out his crews. As a former military officer, he figured I could at least be counted upon to show up on time and put in an honest day's work. Those were his baseline requirements. The rest, he explained, I would learn on the job.

I was hired. Next came the matter of compensation. I had absolutely no idea what a former helicopter-pilot-turned-MBA-candidate fetched in the New England construction market, so I had no problem when the owner declared, "I'll start you at seventeen." *Okay*, I thought. Seventeen thousand for the summer was far less than my peers on Wall Street would make, but I figured I could get by. I was living entirely on borrowed money, so anything that would create a positive cash flow was gravy. That turned out to be a good thing. A few weeks later, I received my first paycheck. Only then did I realize that "seventeen" had meant seventeen *dollars* per *hour.* I would make in one week what my classmates would blow in a single happy hour. Well, life's full of choices. And I was definitely not choosing money.

A couple of days later, I was back on my bike, pedaling to my first job site. I was to join a crew building an addition to a historic Watertown farmhouse. I made the five-mile ride from Cambridge without any difficulty, enjoying some fresh, early summer, New England air along the way. Upon arriving on site, I asked the first person I encountered where to find the foreman. Even at that early hour, the place was swarming with activity, and it took me a few minutes to finally get pointed in the right direction. Dodging the reaching, mechanical arms of hydraulic excavators, I worked my way around the perimeter of the structure to the back side of what was to be the new kitchen. Inside, standing among the studs and particle boards, I found my new boss, Vinh.

I didn't know whether Vinh was his first or last name. To everyone who knew him, he was just Vinh. He was a five-foot-tall, Vietnamese immigrant and considered one of the firm's best foremen. He had served as an officer in the South Vietnamese Army and had spent several years in a communist re-education camp in North Vietnam following the 1975 fall of Saigon. Vinh had lost everything in Vietnam—his family, his home, and his identity. I had studied the Vietnam conflict fairly extensively and had read widely of the plight of American pilots shot down and imprisoned in the infamous *Hanoi Hilton*. That Vinh had survived a similar ordeal and gone on to build an entirely new life in the US earned him my immediate and lasting respect.

I quickly understood why Vinh was considered such an outstanding foreman. In addition to him being a highly accomplished carpenter, he was the master choreographer of a dozen different subcontractors. He skillfully sequenced work to ensure there was absolutely no slack time on the job site. Vinh continually thought three and four steps ahead, barking orders into his cell phone to time the arrival of material and men at precisely the right moments. It was truly a thing of beauty. He would have been a great air boss on an aircraft carrier.

Vinh was an exacting professional, but with a wicked sense of humor. We quickly hit it off after he learned of my military background, and I soon discovered the lighter side of Vinh's all-business persona. He had numerous Vinh-isms that kept everyone on the site continually entertained. My favorite was his threat to publicly execute anyone who made even the simplest mistake.

"You know what happen you forget to bring nails to roof?" he would ask, a look of stone-sober seriousness on his face.

"No, Vinh. What happens?" I knew what was coming, but I'd nevertheless play along.

"*Die before dawn . . .*" he'd reply.

That was his all-time favorite line. He wouldn't provide any details as to how one might die, only the promise that one's life would be ended some time in the early morning hours due to one's transgression. He loved saying that. And he didn't limit his threats of execution only to people at the construction site. Even his family members were occasionally at risk.

"You know what happen my wife, she forget to put cheese on sandwich?"

"No, Vinh. What would happen to her?"

"*Die before dawn . . .*"

Vinh was but one member of a highly colorful cast of characters that moved in and out of my experience that summer. Guys with specialty skills would show up at appointed times to complete their respective portions of the project, exposing me to a slice of the American population with which I'd had little to no interaction to that point: the New England construction worker. Few resembled their pedigreed, public-television patriarch, Norm Abram. Rather, the men I encountered represented highly diverse social and ethnic backgrounds, had a wide variety of work and educational experience, and were incredibly good at what they did.

No two looked, acted, or spoke the same. But they all agreed on one thing: if the Red Sox didn't get their shit together, they were going to kill someone.

It was an odd thing. Among Sox fans, it seemed the team could do no right. But to an outsider, the same fans would insist the team could do no wrong. Boston Red Sox fans were both fiercely protective and highly critical of their beloved, frequently despised, hometown team. It was the strange dynamic of a large, dysfunctional family.

I witnessed this dysfunction every morning following a Red Sox loss. Guys would show up on the job site ready to throw punches over whatever they considered the team's most egregious misstep from the previous night. Usually, it had something to do with Manny Ramirez, the Sox' highly talented—frequently lazy—outfielder.

The opening jab would go something like, "You see Manny last night? What the *hell* was that?"

Then, depending on the other guy's appetite for sparring that morning, he might reply with, "I know! Tell me about it . . ." Or, "Hey, you leave Manny out of this!" Sometimes, a guy would be too exasperated to even discuss the matter and would reply with, "I don't wanna talk about it." That was usually met with, "Well, you got no choice. You *have* to talk about it." No true fan was off the hook when it came to dissecting a game or assigning blame to players—especially Ramirez.

I had absolutely no desire to be a Red Sox fan. It would be too cliché, I thought, to be yet another transient Harvard kid who jumped on the bandwagon, particularly after their long-awaited, 2004 World Series win. Too many had already done so, and the locals certainly did not take kindly to it. Plus, let's face it. Red Sox fans were obnoxious. The banter I witnessed every morning at the job site was mildly entertaining, but come on. Get over it.

And then I got hopelessly sucked in. I don't know if it was the result of listening to the guys mix it up every morning or the fact I lived almost directly across the Charles River from Fenway Park and could hear the crowd cheering from my living room on game nights. Whatever the cause, dammit, I became a Red Sox fan. And my wife got sucked in, too. Thus, nearly every night that summer found us on the couch, shouting at the television, cursing Manny Ramirez, along with every other obnoxious fan in New England. We were part of the tribe. I slowly progressed from passively listening to the guys arguing every morning to actively participating. It added new flavor to the experience.

And it's likely that talking baseball gained me acceptance on the job site when my construction skills did not. Vinh had posed two very reasonable questions when I'd met him: "What building experience do you have?" and "What sort of carpentry skills do you possess?" My answers were: "None," and, "None," respectively. We thus both concluded my involvement on the job site would be limited to manual, unskilled labor. And I was fine with that. I dug ditches, carried shingles up ladders, fetched tools, and swept up at the end of the day. There wasn't anything the least bit belittling in this work. I did what I was qualified to do and was content doing it.

But as time went on, Vinh and the other guys started teaching me things. I learned how to frame out a room. I learned how to hang drywall. I insulated an attic. I laid radiant flooring. I learned how to shape exterior window moldings by hand. I installed beautiful, ipe floor planks on a wrap-around porch. And, most satisfying of all, I got to build staircases.

Near the end of the summer, Vinh decided it was time for me to graduate from digging the footings to constructing the stairs themselves. This turned out to be far trickier than I'd imagined, and I fully appreciated why Vinh had waited so long to teach me. Through it all, I learned how to nail straight, saw straight, measure twice, cut once, and gained a level of comfort with power tools I'd never previously enjoyed. I worked outside, with my hands, alongside incredibly skilled artisans, who were as passionate about baseball as they were the quality of their work. Every night, I enjoyed the deep, sound sleep of a person who had the privilege to *work* for a living. It was a profoundly satisfying experience.

To cap off the summer, I elected to do what any responsible, full-time student with a wife, daughter, staggering levels of student loan debt, and no income would do: I took the family for a week's vacation to Bermuda. Even though I hadn't spent the summer on Wall Street, I figured there was no harm in pretending, and spending, as though I had.

I thus began my second and final year at the Harvard Business School well rested, darkly tanned, and in the best shape of my life. I'd had a good summer. But I was no closer to figuring out what the hell I was supposed to do as a civilian.

I had only one clear mission that year: no spreadsheets. The second year afforded students the opportunity to build their own class schedules and focus on whatever areas of business interested them most. Many of my classmates took deep dives into finance, real estate, entrepreneurship, the nonprofit sector, and many other highly targeted, very useful courses of study. Not me. The driving force behind my course selection strategy was my very strong desire to completely avoid Microsoft Excel. If I couldn't do the math in my head, I wasn't interested. Calculator? Maybe. Spreadsheet? Nothing doing.

I thus set out to wander aimlessly through my final months at Harvard. No industry, business function, or company I encountered the first year of business school had piqued my interest or suggested anything that might merit further study. There were a handful of active duty military officers in my class whose services had sponsored their MBAs. I was far more interested in what they had received for follow-on orders than I was in any opportunity my civilian peers were pursuing. Business school felt like just another tour, as though

I'd never left the Navy. I expected the phone to ring any day with a call from the Navy Personnel Command to order me back to sea. While I knew that call wasn't coming, I simply could not get myself interested in studying business or finding a civilian job.

I had thoroughly enjoyed my brief time in residential construction. However, I knew I wasn't moving on to a career as an unskilled laborer. Having spent the summer as one had made me something of a novelty among my classmates and a curiosity among the faculty. Some thought I was an idiot for squandering the golden opportunity that was the Harvard Business School. I can't say I disagreed. Whatever the case, I had apparently waited until business school to hit my rebellious streak. I would not allow myself to follow my much smarter classmates into the highly exclusive, high-paying jobs to which they flocked in droves.

Early in the second semester of my second year, having labored under the illusion the previous eighteen months that this would all work itself out, I started to get stressed. Graduation was looming, and I didn't have a clue as to what the hell I was going to do. Luckily, folks at the career services office had advice beyond just "follow your passion." To narrow your job search, they advised, you must think in terms of industry, function, and geography. In a perfect world, you'd land a position that aligned all three to your interests. If not three, then two. If not two, one.

It worked like this: jazzed about cars? Start having conversations with alumni in the auto industry to figure out which functions were possible fits and where, geographically, opportunities could be found. Done. Or, say you're a numbers person, intrigued by the challenge of optimizing the balance sheets of public companies. That suggested corporate finance as your function, so go hit one of the many hiring conferences on campus to learn about companies looking for talent in that area. Easy day. If you were like me, completely disinterested in any industry or function, you need only decide where you want to live, and then take anything you could find to pay the bills there.

Geography was the one piece of the puzzle I could envision clearly. I wanted to live in San Diego. Badly. The Navy had taken me there numerous times, for both brief and extended stays, and my wife and I had come to love the place. I loved the ocean, the mountains, the desert, the fish tacos, the eclectic neighborhoods, the laid-back vibe . . . everything. Some of our very best friends lived there. And those who didn't would probably be stationed there eventually. I deeply appreciated the city's long, proud history with the United States Navy, to include portions of *Top Gun* having been filmed there. That meant something. And, of course, who couldn't love the weather? San Diego enjoyed perfect sunshine, zero humidity, and a comfortable, seventy-three degrees Fahrenheit 330 days a year. It made you want to go outside, rip off your shirt, and run an Ironman triathlon.

Beyond all the obvious reasons I wanted to live there, San Diego held a very deep, powerful, psychological sway over me. As a kid growing up in Michigan, I watched television shows on Nickelodeon that featured kids riding skateboards in t-shirts and shorts in January somewhere in Southern California. In the depths of a frozen Michigan winter, I wanted nothing more than to be one of those kids. It wasn't just that I hated winter, which I absolutely did. But I came to define success as the means to extricate oneself from the small-town Midwest and relocate to an area with palm trees, sunshine, and surf. Success was California. Failure was Michigan. It had everything to do with why I'd enlisted in the Navy and left all those years before.

I was therefore anxious to meet one of the subjects of my independent research project. One of the more productive choices I'd made that second year was to conduct an independent study of risk and entrepreneurship. I'd harbored a feeling that fifteen years in the military had made me risk-averse. There had been very few life decisions I'd had to make on my own, and my entire career had been largely scripted. I'd lived in base housing, shopped in on-base commissaries, and hung out exclusively with military people my entire adult life. Under such circumstances, I wondered if maybe there were opportunities I was afraid to seize without the guiding hand of Mother Navy to lead the way. To find out, I enlisted the help of my entrepreneurship professor to gain a view of risk through the eyes of those who enjoyed a very intimate understanding of it: small-business owners and Navy SEALs.

With my professor's help, and through my own Navy contacts, I assembled a group of research subjects with whom I conducted a series of in-depth interviews. Without exception, these were some of the most fascinating conversations I'd had in my entire life. One of my business school classmates, himself a former SEAL officer, described in detail the time he and a couple of teammates maneuvered a SEAL Delivery Vehicle beneath the hull of a moving aircraft carrier as it transited a narrow strait, just to prove it could be done. SEAL Delivery Vehicles, or SDVs, are mini-submarines Navy Special Warfare Operators use to reconnoiter bad-guy beaches and harbors. At one point, my buddy estimated the SDV had no more than five feet of clearance beneath the massive, 100,000-ton war ship. Now that was some serious risk.

And what had he taken from the experience?

"It was an incredibly stupid idea," he said.

Turns out, he had allowed himself to be talked into it by the senior enlisted man on his team, despite his every instinct not to do it. In my friend's estimate, the potential benefit simply did not outweigh the potential cost. What was an extra dose of bravado in light of the very real possibility the team would be crushed and killed? While he and his teammates had pulled it off, my buddy resolved thenceforth to trust his instincts and stand his ground. These very qualities later served him extremely well when he found himself squarely in the middle of some of the most intense fighting in the Iraqi conflict.

Risk for risk's sake is irrational. But if the objective is compelling enough, one will instinctively accept, manage, and mitigate risk to achieve that objective. That was the key finding of my study and very much the view of Greg, the Navy officer turned small-business owner

I met the next-to-last day of spring break. Greg owned a couple of web sites, through which he ran a successful retail business that provided him a very comfortable lifestyle in northern San Diego County. He had been self-employed for most of his time since leaving the Navy, had taken his licks as a small-business owner, and had found a way to make it work. I thought I could learn a few things from Greg and was grateful a mutual friend had made an introduction.

We met at a coffee shop near the beach. Greg looked every bit the Southern California entrepreneur—tan, fit, and shaggy haired, wearing designer jeans and flip-flops. We struck an immediate, comfortable rapport. I don't know what he thought of me, but I liked him. As we worked through the series of questions I'd prepared for my research project, an enjoyable conversation ensued that eventually found its way to the topic of my post-graduation plans. I shared how unimpressed I'd been with everything to which I'd been exposed in business school, my very strong desire to live in San Diego, and my uncertainty as to how to proceed. Greg nodded along, admitting he found it a bit puzzling someone with such a wide variety of opportunities laid before him could find none of them appealing. If nothing the Harvard Business School made possible impressed me, what would?

As we talked it through, an idea began to take shape. Yes, Greg's was a small business. But with the right business partner, perhaps it could grow. Maybe what he needed was a young, hungry, fellow Naval officer with a strong desire not to follow the herd and a solid-platinum MBA in his back pocket. While business school hadn't inspired me, I had at least resolved to get my money's worth and absorbed all the lessons I could on how to make an organization successful. I felt I had something to offer Greg, whether he realized it or not. I thus steered the conversation in the direction of *his* future. Was he satisfied with the current state of his business? What were his long-term objectives? Had he fully exploited opportunities in the markets he currently served? Could he make a play into new markets? Was he fully leveraging his brand to create maximum value?

Of course, I had no practical experience whatsoever on which to draw to provide answers to any of these questions. But, through the course of the MBA program, I'd studied hundreds of companies that had wrestled with these issues. Greg seemed to enjoy having someone to challenge his thinking on both the current and future states of his business. He seemed to value the dialogue and back-and-forth exchange of ideas. While Greg had the view from the trenches and could speak from direct experience, I'd had access to some of the greatest business thinkers in the entire world and had been taught all the *right* answers, to the extent that there were any. We had a terrific conversation that lasted more than two hours. At the end, I decided to make a move. I slid a copy of my resume across the table and told Greg that together, we could take his business to an entirely new level. And we shouldn't waste any time. I said he should hire me immediately, so we could get started right after graduation. It was an uncharacteristically gutsy move on my part.

I could tell by Greg's reaction I'd caught him off guard. He hadn't expected our conversation to take a turn in that direction. Still, it was obvious he was intrigued. When you run a small business, he explained, hiring decisions are hugely consequential. A bad hire could literally bust you. But maybe, he thought, the right person could help him achieve things with his business that he could not attain alone. And maybe that person was indeed me.

We left the coffee shop with a mutual commitment to continue the conversation. The next day, I was on a plane headed back to Boston, certain I'd just hit the jackpot. I had unearthed exactly the right opportunity, with exactly the right person, in exactly the right place, at exactly the right time. I had sensed an opening and taken decisive action. It was all coming together.

And indeed it did. Two weeks later, Greg extended me an offer that, despite placing me in the bottom tenth percentile among my classmates for starting salaries, gave me my ticket to San Diego. I was ecstatic. Later that June, diploma in hand, my family and I made the move. *See*, I told myself. *It paid to not follow the herd. Wall Street was for suckers.*

Until, that is, *I* was made the sucker.

Four months after the move to San Diego, I was fired. I turned out to be exactly the costly, bad hire Greg had described in our first conversation. It wasn't that we hadn't gotten along. Rather, I didn't fetch Greg the immediate return on investment he needed to justify paying me.

"I think it's time to end the experiment," he said.

Nice, I thought. *This has all been a goddamned experiment to you?*

But what an experiment! Working for Greg meant you showed up late, wore jeans and flip-flops, spent two hours working out, and then went home early. In between, maybe you did some work, but certainly nothing strenuous.

I remember my Dad's assessment of my situation when I described it to him a few weeks after I'd started. "You're living in a fantasy world," he'd said, "and it will not last."

"Come on, Dad. You're just being old-fashioned."

More telling was a comment made by one of Greg's acquaintances, a venture capital guy who stopped by the office one evening. When I asked him whether Greg should be hitting up the Southern California investment community for growth funding, the guy nearly shot the Diet Coke he was drinking out of his nose.

"Are you kidding me? No frickin' way. You can't scale this thing."

So there I was. Six months after graduating from the Harvard Business School, I was unemployed, with a family to support, up to my eyeballs in student loan debt, living in one of the most expensive cities in the country, with zero prospects.

This was where my passion had led me.

LESSONS LEARNED

1. The pursuit of passion is a fool's errand. It's a swing-for-the-fences approach to career planning that can and will fail. Some people have an all-consuming, singular interest, the pursuit of which pays the bills. But most of us do not. We have to figure it out through trial and error. And that's okay.

2. Be smart about the trials, and work to minimize the negative impacts of the errors. Do this by seeking roles that enable you to build useful skills, gain wide exposure to different functions and industries, and pay well. Just because you haven't discovered your passion doesn't mean you can't build a solid resume, improve your finances, and be a useful human being.

3. You don't have to follow the herd. But if a large group of smart, successful, highly talented people gravitates in a certain direction, understand why.

   My business school classmates flocked to top-tier investment banks and management consulting firms after graduation. I thought they wanted to be bankers and consultants. Wrong. They understood those firms to be springboards to other, more interesting, more lucrative opportunities that were more in line with their true interests. Most did a tour and then moved on, with stronger resumes, professional networks, skills, and bank accounts.

   Rather than "Follow your passion," I really wish someone in the career services office had instead told me to, "Shut the fuck up, and go be a consultant!"

How Not to Be the New Guy

"What is up *with Dan?"*

Orlando, Florida, 2008.

O f all the outcomes I could have imagined following my Harvard graduation, unemployment wasn't one of them. But there I was. And it was a condition I had to remedy— quickly.

So I talked to a friend, who knew a guy, who'd heard of a retired Navy officer who might have an opportunity. I networked my way to a meeting, which led to a discussion with a recruiter, then a couple rounds of interviews, and, finally, an offer. Done.

The tricky thing was, while I'd made my desire to remain in San Diego clear, the human resources director of the public sector consulting firm I'd just joined had made it equally clear that the majority of my work would require that I be in Washington, DC. And the firm would pay for neither travel nor relocation from west coast to east. *Fine*, I thought. *Just give me a paycheck, and I'll sort the rest out later.*

I made my way east and promptly imposed upon various friends in and around DC, whose basements and guestrooms I occupied for too long, ruining some long-standing, meaningful relationships in the process. All the while, my wife and daughter remained in limbo in San Diego, not knowing whether they were staying or moving. So while I was no longer unemployed, the situation was far from ideal.

But it could have been worse. I could have been the guy in the frog suit.

It was late-May and about a thousand degrees on the golf course. My job was to drive a cart from hole to hole, so Freddy the Frog, seated next to me, could wave at the golfers. It was also my job to provide John, the guy wearing the Freddy costume, a sufficient supply of water and Gatorade to ward off heat exhaustion. Out on the golf course, riding around in a full-body, polyester frog suit provided the same benefit as wearing a snowmobile suit on a forced march through an Ecuadorian jungle.

Freddy was the mascot some colonel had dreamt up for the Pentagon directorate he led. John and I worked for the firm that provided various administrative support services to that directorate. Somehow, those services included having John and me patrol a Central Florida golf course to provide entertainment for the hundred or so mid-grade officers who'd traveled there for the directorate's annual convention. The golf tournament was one of the marquee events, and the colonel wanted Freddy everywhere, strutting and waving, inviting every possible photo op. And there were surprisingly many. I couldn't believe the number of people who wanted their picture taken with that frog. I was embarrassed for them.

I was thirty-four years old, a Naval Academy graduate, a former Naval aviator, and held a Harvard MBA. John was in his late twenties, a Georgetown graduate, and had just been accepted to the Johns Hopkins University School of Medicine. One would be hard pressed to find two people more overqualified for a given task. John had been with the consulting firm a year longer than I, and only because I was four inches taller and didn't fit into the frog suit were our roles not reversed. We endured the heat, the frog suit, and the absurdity of the whole affair, because it was better than sitting behind a desk in the Pentagon—and we were both only days away from leaving the firm. John was departing to enjoy some time off before starting medical school. I was leaving because I'd had it. Recent events had led me to conclude driving Freddy the Frog around was not a one-off event. This was to be my lot in the organization.

For the record, I know what it is to pay one's dues. In my time in the Navy, I had played the role of recruit, plebe, pollywog, nugget, second pilot, FNG (a squadron term for Fucking New Guy), and about a dozen other new-kid, bottom-of-the-pile bits that required I shut up, swallow my pride, and take a beating. I had scrubbed toilets, swabbed decks, and chipped paint. I had been made to wallow in a kiddie pool full of Crisco, paraded around in my underwear to the amusement of various audiences, and jogged the length of an Oahu beach in an under-sized Speedo and Tina Turner wig. I'd been arbitrarily given mind-numbingly boring jobs, devoid of any interest or challenge, which I never would have chosen for myself. I'd had to accept that to advance, I would have to pass through the Navy's mandatory wickets and wait my turn to be given an opportunity. I'd endured all of this because I believed deeply in the goodness of the organization, the tremendous quality of its people, and the nobility of the purpose they served. Plus, on many occasions, there may have been more than a little alcohol involved.

Given my distinguished body of work in this area, one may wonder why I was so put out to have to pay my dues this time around. It had to do with a conversation I'd overheard the week before. I had joined a conference call a few minutes late. Not wanting to interrupt the discussion, I didn't bother announcing myself. As such, neither Jill, my immediate boss, nor Andrew, the overall lead for the engagement, knew I was listening. At the end of the call, Andrew asked Jill to remain on the line. He wanted to talk to her about me.

Jill and I had gotten along fairly well. I had done everything she'd asked of me and enjoyed a terrific rapport with each of our Pentagon clients, including a deputy assistant secretary. That was good for her, good for me, and good for the firm. My duties weren't terribly strenuous, but I thought I'd done respectable work for Jill to that point. Andrew was the up-and-coming engagement manager with whom I'd been teamed to ensure my early experience with the firm was positive. He was considered one of the firm's best—definite partner material. Andrew wasn't a terrible guy, but I found him a touch self-important. Once, while running thirty minutes late for a meeting he had scheduled, he remarked with notable satisfaction, "I don't mind having people wait on me."

While the others who'd been on the conference call checked off, I took a moment to weigh the risks of eavesdropping on a private conversation between my two superiors. On the one hand, if I was ever discovered to have been on the line, I'd most certainly be fired. On the other, I'd already had the rug pulled out from underneath me by Greg back in San Diego, and there had been immediate, negative financial consequences for me and my family. There was no way I was about to let that happen again. Thus, if my eavesdropping produced actionable intelligence on my future employment with the organization, it was a risk worth taking. So I did.

Andrew began, "So what is *up* with Dan?"

"I know!" Jill immediately replied.

He went on, "I mean, who does he think he is? He acts all important, because he spends all his time with Clark."

Mr. Clark was our client, a deputy assistant secretary. He was a former Army officer, and we'd hit it off immediately.

"Meanwhile, he hasn't done a thing with the virtual PMO."

The virtual PMO, or Project Management Office, was Andrew's brainchild. Most engagements required a dedicated junior analyst to track project hours and expenses, prepare client billing, and perform other low-level administrative tasks. In this case, the client had refused to pay for what it viewed as unnecessary overhead, so we had no junior analyst. The various duties were spread among the other consultants. Andrew wanted to build an online, shareable database to serve as a repository for hours and expenses, which would then be fed back to the central office for client billing. This would serve as his *virtual* project manager.

I thought the whole thing redundant and a complete waste of time. The firm already had a system that performed exactly the functions Andrew desired for his virtual PMO. He nonetheless wanted his own system and had decided I was to be its architect. And until it was up and running, I was also to assume the duties of the junior analyst. This had all shaken out my first week on the project, and I'd done only the minimum necessary to give the appearance I was making any progress. I thought my time was better spent doing quality work for clients.

Andrew continued, "He just refuses to *step up* and do what a new kid's supposed to do." He was pretty angry. It was clear his frustration with my apparent insubordination had been building for some time.

Jill was in complete agreement. In a sinister tone, she replied, "Well . . . we can fix that."

Andrew and Jill then decided that every petty, menial, mundane, entry-level task they could possibly come up with would be given to me. It was to be a test. Either I would get the message, check my huge ego, and fall in line, or I'd leave the firm. Preferably, they both agreed, I would do the latter.

When the call ended, I just sat there for a while, hands shaking, completely bewildered. I had *never* heard anyone talk that way about me. Never. Especially a boss. I couldn't have imagined a more appalling scenario.

The partner who'd hired me, Andrew's boss, had said she was thrilled to have a former military officer and MBA join the firm. She'd said my intelligence, communication skills, and highly polished, professional demeanor would enable Andrew to put me in front of the firm's most important clients right away. She'd said my military background would give me credibility other consultants lacked. She'd said my experience working closely with senior officers would make me an immediate, high-demand asset. She'd said . . . She'd said . . . She'd said . . .

Andrew didn't subscribe to any of that. I was the new kid, and I was going to pay my dues. It was just that simple.

The call had taken place on a Friday afternoon. First thing Monday morning, Jill paid me a visit. She'd always been cordial with me. Not anymore. She curtly dumped half a dozen tasks in my lap and directed that I check in with her at various points throughout the day to inform her of my progress with them. The *run-Dan-out-of-the-firm* plan was in full effect.

Unbeknownst to Andrew and Jill, I was doing everything I could to ensure their plan's success. As far as I was concerned, there was nothing salvageable in this situation. Even if matters improved with Andrew and Jill, I'd lost all respect for them. Likewise, I'd lost all faith in the organization that had chosen to elevate such people to positions of leadership. I didn't believe in the work, and I could see all the promises I'd been made by the partner who'd hired me were completely empty. Thus, I'd already spoken to a headhunter and expected to have interviews lined up by the following week. In the meantime, I would happily accept my new tasks, report promptly and thoroughly on their completion, and dive eagerly into the virtual PMO. I would give every appearance I was a fully committed team player. I would be the model new kid, cheerfully paying my dues, just as Andrew wanted.

The headhunter moved even faster than I'd anticipated. I took a vacation day the following Monday to fly out for an interview. That Wednesday, I received an offer. Two days later, I was on the Orlando golf course, driving around Freddy the Frog. Rather than give Jill or Andrew the satisfaction of receiving my two weeks' notice, I instead called the partner who'd hired me to inform her I was leaving.

Regardless of how or when they received the news, I'm sure Andrew and Jill were thrilled.

LESSONS LEARNED

1. Dues paid in the military count for nothing in the private sector. That was a hard lesson. My mettle had been tested in situations far more challenging, by leaders far more seasoned, and I had proven myself capable. But none of that mattered. Who the hell was I to blow off my boss? Nothing in my military experience entitled me to such insubordination. A more mature and emotionally intelligent person would have recognized this and simply paid his dues. Or, he at least would have done what his boss told him to do. I lacked the patience, and humility, to do either.

2. But it's awfully hard to pay your dues when you have *zero* respect for your boss, your boss's boss, your work, and your organization. That was mostly my fault. I had unrealistically high expectations of this employer, based upon very limited information. I should have chosen far more carefully. Ten minutes of due diligence on my part would have likely revealed this role to be a very poor fit. Unfortunately, I'd needed a job, quickly, and had not conducted a proper investigation. I'd allowed myself to rush to a bad decision.

3. Andrews and Jills are everywhere. Whatever their qualifications, they're usually petty, insecure, and territorial. They're incredibly shitty bosses. And when I encounter an Andrew or a Jill, my first inclination is to ignore them. But that's not an effective strategy.

    Not all bosses ascend to positions of leadership because they're qualified to lead. Some have deep expertise in a certain area and are put in charge of people with similar expertise.

Others have simply been around longer than anyone else. And some are put in charge, because no one else is willing to accept the responsibility.

Whatever the case, they're the boss. So, you have two choices: find a way to make it work or leave.

Aviate, Navigate, Communicate

"We may end up in the Hudson."

Corporate America, 2008.

I discovered a curious phenomenon during the Great Recession: it's far more stressful to *pretend* to work than it is to actually work. And when you don't know what the hell you're supposed to be doing, you do a lot of pretending.

I couldn't blame the headhunter. When I first called him, seeking to escape Andrew and Jill, all the guidance I provided was, "make it Fortune 500 in a low-cost-of-living area." And when he came back with an opportunity for a role that didn't sound the least bit interesting, with a company about which I cared nothing, in a part of the country I would have otherwise avoided, my response was, "Whatever. I'll take it."

And then, only weeks after arriving, the entire world economy was on the verge of collapse.

Heads were rolling. Every morning, there'd be another empty cubicle. I remember one day I heard a loud, sudden gasp from a woman a few rows over. Several colleagues and I immediately rushed to the sound, thinking the woman was having a heart attack. When we arrived on the scene, we found her stretched out on the floor. She'd just been informed her position had been eliminated. The paramedics rolled her out on a gurney. We later learned the woman had not, thankfully, had a heart attack. Instead, her collapse to the floor had been a psychosomatic response to the news of the loss of her job.

It was the same scene playing out at companies across the country. Customers were cancelling orders, production was slowing, and organizations were in full cost-cutting mode as a result. People were expensive. So, naturally, headcount reductions were central to the *trough plans* of many companies. The unnerving thing was, whatever logic determined whose head was to be cut was unknown to the masses, so the firings seemed random and arbitrary. Maybe you were a key player who would survive the downturn. Or, more likely, you were expendable. You just didn't know.

Either way, it was time to hunker down and look busy. That proved to be a challenge, because I was working for a guy who absolutely refused to provide my coworkers and me with any meaningful direction.

Most of us were recently retired or separated from the active duty military, still finding our footing in this strange, new, corporate world. The boss had been a long-time consultant and was best buddies with the guy who headed our group. Early on, he'd called a meeting in which he intended, he claimed, to explain the purpose of our group and the value it was meant to create for the organization. *Perfect*, we all thought. But then he walked into the conference room, threw a thick, littered binder on the table, said, "Read it," and then walked right back out. My colleagues and I opened the binder and found it mostly comprised of outdated technical memoranda. After half an hour of head-scratching, we left the room more confused than we'd been when we'd walked in.

"I hire smart people and let them figure out what they're supposed to do," the boss proudly explained.

If you tried to coax anything that even resembled guidance out of him, he'd look at you like you were stupid and say, "Just figure it out." Having hired you, a supposedly *smart person*, he was thereby relieved from any burden to further guide and develop you. If you were unable to do those things on your own, well, you must not be so smart after all.

Having no idea whether your livelihood was in jeopardy, but having to assume it was, created strong incentive to continuously demonstrate your value to the organization. And since you had no idea what the hell you might do to create that value, all you could do was fake it. That meant you had to come in early. Put your butt in a chair. Clatter away on your computer. Shout into a phone. Always be seen carrying a clipboard. Be in a rush wherever you went. Have a pissed-off look on your face. And then leave late. It was like that Seinfeld episode in which George gets agitated every time he encounters Mr. Wilhelm to give the impression he's busy. "George, you're working too hard!" Precisely.

What a waste! At a time when the organization needed its best and brightest laser-focused on those few, critically important matters that would enable it to survive the economic downturn, most were instead wasting away their hours on trivial activities, growing increasingly anxious, bored, confused, and frustrated in the process. It was dysfunctional. None of us needed to have his hand held, but a little clear direction would have gone a long way toward relieving the anxiety. It would have enabled us to confine our efforts to value-additive activities that materially benefited the company, the group, and ourselves. If ultimately the business failed, at least then we would have felt more in control of our destinies, doing whatever we could to affect a positive outcome, rather than merely left to the whims of fate.

Fortunately, the business did not fail. It survived, as did our group. The only casualty was our lazy-ass boss. He was fired. I wanted to think his inability to define objectives and set priorities was enough to get him terminated. But, apparently, sexually harassing women and expensing boxes of Cuban cigars did the trick instead.

Faking my way through the Great Recession made me appreciate an important lesson from my flying days: just as a lack of clear direction and priorities prevents both people and organizations from realizing their full, value-creating potential—the opposite is also true. Their presence unleashes tremendous drive and creative energy, enabling members to march in step toward the most important outcomes—the critical few. Because these priorities, properly defined, drive desired behaviors throughout the entire organization, they must be set with great care. So how do you do that? How do you set that North Star that guides all your sailors?

Think of leading a team like flying a plane: first, aviate; then, navigate; finally, communicate.

From the first day of Navy flight training, students were taught how to diagnose and manage a variety of in-flight emergencies. In fact, you spend so much time studying and practicing emergency procedures, you began to think Navy aircraft must be falling out of the sky on a regular basis.

Of course, they were not. On a typical day, you'd show up, brief your flight, walk to the aircraft, pre-flight, spin it up, launch, and then go do touch-and-gos at some outlying field or practice maneuvers over some patch of rural, North Florida swamp land. The student sat in the front seat and the instructor in the back. The student's job was to *aeronautically adapt* and become proficient enough in the prescribed procedures and maneuvers to progress to the next phase of training and, ultimately, earn the Wings of Gold. The instructor's job was to harass and frustrate the student every step of the way.

There was good reason for that. Naval aviators operate in some tough environments. How can you handle getting shot at, for example, if you can't handle getting smacked around a little by a flight instructor? Learning to manage stress in the cockpit was core to the Navy flight training experience and, I'll admit, proved useful on those dark, no-visible-horizon nights when it was a chore just to find, let alone land on, a pitching flight deck in the middle of the ocean.

With all that was required, or could be required, of a pilot on any given flight, it was critical to have a clear set of priorities. And before you even zipped on a flight suit for the first time, those priorities were beaten into you: aviate, navigate, communicate. First, fly the plane. Second, fly it in the right direction. Last, talk to people outside the plane—air traffic controllers, other pilots, etc.

Instructors had an effective way of driving the point home. You'd be out tooling around the operating area, working on a turn pattern or some other trivial maneuver, and then, all of a sudden, you'd hear the engine start winding down. The nose would pitch downward, and the sound of wind rushing past the fuselage would get louder as the aircraft started losing altitude. You'd look down and see the throttle pulled all the way back to idle, at which time the instructor would announce from the back seat, "Simulated" (the aircraft had an identical set of controls in the back seat, which instructors used to wreak all sorts of havoc on students). It was their way of informing you that you'd just experienced a simulated engine failure and should promptly execute the proper emergency procedure.

Even when you knew it was coming, it somehow caught you by surprise. And the moment you got your wits about you and started working the problem, the instructor would invariably chime in from the back seat and pretend to be the air traffic controller, "Six Echo Two Three Six, hold you twenty-five miles northwest, passing angels four-point-five. Assigned altitude is angels five. Are you experiencing any difficulty?"

As a student, my reply went something like, "Uh . . . maybe. Possible engine failure. Troubleshooting now."

The instructor would then continue, "Two Three Six, are you declaring an emergency?"

Confused, I would then reply, "Uh . . . no?" And then the instructor would continue, "Roger. Turn to new course two-seven-zero."

And then, without understanding why, I would dutifully repeat, "Roger, two-seven-zero," and turn the plane.

Having thus taken the bait, the instructor would continue this back-and-forth with me for several seconds while I did my best to talk and execute my procedures at the same time. Eventually, the instructor, playing the role of controller, would have me doing nine things at once, riding the unicycle while juggling bowling pins and reciting the Gettysburg Address, all while the aircraft continued to lose altitude.

There was a name for this condition: *helmet fire*. You could almost see the smoke emanating from underneath a student's helmet as his brain sparked and sputtered to process too much information at once.

When the instructor thought you'd had enough, you would hear the words of defeat, "I have the controls." That meant your helmet fire was burning brightly enough for the instructor to consider it prudent to assume control of the aircraft. They'd level off, give you a moment to get your wits about you, and then tell you what you already knew: you'd lost all situational awareness and abandoned your priorities in the process.

"*Never* stop flying the plane," they'd say. "Don't let a controller, or anyone else, distract you from your first priority."

If you want to know what right looks like in this situation, look no further than US Airways flight 1549, the *Miracle on the Hudson*.

Shortly after 3:25 p.m. Eastern Standard Time on January 15, 2009, Captain Chesley "Sully" Sullenberger and 154 others departed New York's LaGuardia Airport for Charlotte. By 3:31 p.m., the aircraft and all 155 occupants were floating in the Hudson River off Manhattan, having sustained only minimal damage and injuries. Only seconds after takeoff, flight 1549 encountered an unfortunate flock of Canadian geese, most of which was ingested by the aircraft engines, causing both to fail.

Sully and his copilot, Jeffrey Skiles, had very few options. They'd reached an altitude of only 3,000 feet, all but eliminating their chance to glide the plane to a nearby runway. Sully quickly decided the least bad of any remaining options was to ditch in the frigid Hudson.

This all took place in a matter of seconds. During that time, the conversation between Sully and Patrick Harten, the controller at New York Terminal Radar Approach Control, was textbook.

Sullenberger (15:27:32.9): "Mayday, mayday, mayday. Uh, this is, uh, Cactus Fifteen Thirty-Nine. Hit birds. We've lost thrust in both engines. We're turning back towards LaGuardia."

LaGuardia Departure Control (15:27:42): "Okay, uh, you need to return to LaGuardia? Turn left heading of, uh, two-two-zero."

LaGuardia Departure control (15:28:05): "Cactus Fifteen Twenty-Nine, if we can get it for you do you want to try to land runway one three?"

Sullenberger (15:28:10.6): "We're unable. We may end up in the Hudson."

LaGuardia Departure Control (15:28:31): "Alright Cactus Fifteen Forty-Nine, it's gonna be left traffic for runway three one."

Sullenberger (15:28:35): "Unable."

LaGuardia Departure Control (15:28:36): "Okay, what do you need to land?"

LaGuardia Departure Control (15:28:46): "Cactus Fifteen Twenty-Nine, runway four's available if you wanna make left traffic to runway four."

Sullenberger (15:28:49.9): "I'm not sure we can make any runway. Uh, what's over to our right? Anything in New Jersey, maybe Teterboro?"

LaGuardia Departure Control (15:28:55): "Okay, yeah, off your right side is Teterboro airport."

LaGuardia Departure Control (15:29:02): "You wanna try and go to Teterboro?"

Sullenberger (15:29:03): "Yes."

LaGuardia Departure Control (15:29:21): "Cactus Fifteen Twenty-Nine, turn right two-eight-zero. You can land runway one at Teterboro."

Sullenberger (15:29:25): "We can't do it."

LaGuardia Departure Control (15:29:27): "'Kay, which runway would you like at Teterboro?"

Sullenberger (15:29:28): "We're gonna be in the Hudson."

LaGuardia Departure Control (15:29:33): "I'm sorry, say again, Cactus?"

LaGuardia Departure Control (15:29:53): "Cactus Fifteen Forty-Nine, radar contact is lost, you also got Newark airport off your two o'clock in about seven miles."

Radio from another plane (15:30:09): "Two one zero, uh, forty-seven eighteen. I think he said he's going in the Hudson."

LaGuardia Departure Control (15:30:22): "Cactus Fifteen Twenty-Nine, if you can, uh . . . you got, uh, runway, uh, two nine available at Newark. It'll be two o'clock and seven miles."

This was a noteworthy exchange for a few reasons. First, while most communication between pilots and controllers is brief and to-the-point, particularly in airspace as busy as New York's, this was especially so. Sully exercised maximum brevity, even containing his remarks to a single word when possible. Left traffic for runway three one? "Unable." Beautiful. More flying, less talking.

Second, it's important to note Sullenberger didn't completely ignore the air traffic controller. Rather, he skillfully co-opted him in the problem-solving process *while he continued to fly the plane.* The transcript of the internal conversation between Sullenberger and Skiles reveals the two pilots' methodically working through emergency procedures and developing options for a safe landing, pulling the controller into the conversation only to further develop those options.

Finally, the controller, for his part, did a nice job of providing information that broadened the situational awareness of the pilots rather than detract from it. "Newark airport at your two o'clock in about seven miles." That's useful. While the controller couldn't fly the plane for Sullenberger and Skiles, he could at least give the pilots the information they needed to point the nose in the direction of a clear runway.

Aviate, navigate, communicate. It's a simple, powerful tool pilots use to stay focused on the right things, make good decisions, and keep safe. Shouldn't every employee in every organization be similarly equipped?

Absolutely. But what do they get instead? SMART Goals.

They're all the rage. These rules dictate that an employee's role, and the basis for their incentive compensation, should be defined by a set of objectives that are Specific, Measurable, Achievable, Relevant, and Time-Bound, or SMART. None of that squishy, fully-optimize-organizational-outcomes-to-achieve-target-synergies stuff allowed. This philosophy says that every employee's set of individual objectives should align directly with those of the CEO via the process of cascading. Broader, organizational-level aims are handed down successively through the chain of command and continually refined and tailored to align and maximize individuals' contributions.

In the end, when SMART goals are done correctly and Earnings Per Share ticked up a basis point, every person in the organization, from the C-Suite to the mail room, could point to a specific, pre-ordained task they had completed that had driven and enabled that outcome. Makes imminent sense, right?

But, alas, in too many organizations, SMART goals are anything but. I recently pulled my SMART goals greatest hits from my corporate archives. Not pretty.

(The names of the organizations for which these were derived have been removed to protect the identities of the woefully un-SMART.)

- Support the Director of (organization) via special projects and assignments that enhance and illuminate the value of (organization) to internal and external stakeholders.
- Create metrics that capture trends by region, industry, and focus-area and organize in a manner that clearly and succinctly illustrates to leadership the extent to which strategic objectives are being met.

- Be a valued resource to the (organization). Support colleagues by being an always-available source of information and assistance.
- Assist the (organization) Director, as needed and appropriate, with the implementation of action plans based on employee opinion survey results with emphasis on leadership and engagement elements.
- Understand and abide by (organization's) anti-bribery policies, procedures, and risks. Ensure 100 percent completion of code of conduct and associated required trainings.
- Contribute to an energizing climate. Develop action plans for improvement.

Is this what bosses are passing off as guidance these days? Shit, I hope not. If you want to set goals that actually drive behaviors that get results, make them truly smart. And ensure they focus on *leading*, not *lagging* indicators.

A leading indicator, by my definition, is a metric employees can directly influence through their actions *right now*. They are the needles that move when employees pull the levers immediately available to them. And, as those needles move, they influence or predict the movement of other needles elsewhere in the organization, which represent the lagging indicators. These are the metrics tied to the broader outcomes the company seeks to achieve, such as improved earnings.

In practical terms, ask a machine operator what he's focused on during any given shift and he's going to speak in terms of leading indicators—numbers of widgets produced, per unit time, to certain specifications, at an acceptable level of quality. On the other hand, ask the chief financial officer on any given day what she's focused on, and she's likely to speak in terms of lagging indicators—the resulting impact to the company's financial condition *over time* stemming from the collective ability of the employees to produce and sell those widgets.

Now, if you're the CFO, it probably makes sense for your performance to be measured by the movement of lagging indicators. These measure outcomes at the enterprise level, where an executive's scope of responsibility is more likely to reside. But, farther down the food chain, lagging indicators are far less meaningful. Still, I have observed too many instances of organizational fixation on all things lagging across all levels of a company. And the inevitable result has been that employees have felt completely detached from those things that purportedly defined the company's success and, often, determined their level of incentive compensation. Annual goal setting, for too many organizations, is nothing more than a meaningless box-checking exercise to which employees devote as little time as possible. And why should they?

Setting and communicating clear objectives and priorities that drive long-term value creation takes considerable effort. But it's well worth it. Good bosses make that effort. They clearly define an organization's aviate-navigate-communicate and ensure every member is focused on those leading-indicator activities that drive the most important lagging-indicator outcomes. And he continuously communicates those priorities and the *why* behind them at every opportunity.

A mentor once told me I'd know when I'd begun to effectively communicate my priorities when I started getting sick of hearing myself repeat them. I think that's exactly right.

Don't ever make your employees have to *pretend* to work.

LESSONS LEARNED

1. Employees should never have to wonder what's most important, especially in times of uncertainty. They risk wasting valuable time and imagination on unproductive activities. If you're the boss, don't assume people have figured out the priorities. You must tell them, clearly and repeatedly.

2. Don't over-complicate your goals and priorities. Fewer is better. Succinct is better. Make them understandable, memorable, and quotable. Aviate, navigate, communicate.

3. For the love of God, if you're going to require your employees to write SMART goals, please ensure they're actually *smart* and designed to drive the proper, leading-indicator behaviors.

Having a Bad Day? Your Boss Thinks It's PTSD

"I want you to know I'm proud of you
. . . for getting *help*."

Corporate America, 2010.

My boss was convinced I was suffering from Post-Traumatic Stress Disorder.

I had just returned from a year-long sabbatical in Kuwait, compliments of the United States Navy Reserve. During that time, I had helped oversee the safe delivery of more than twelve million tons of ammunition and explosives to two combat theaters of operation. I had led a watch team that coordinated security and counter-terror efforts to ensure the safety of more than 300 US service personnel. And I had worked closely with the US Naval attaché to strengthen ties with the Kuwaitis, among our most critical allies in one of the most important regions to US national security. It had been a very busy, highly rewarding year in which I had been sharply focused, continually engaged, and completely committed to the mission's success.

The same could not be said of the situation to which I'd returned. Prior to deployment, I had been working in corporate public affairs. I'd been hired the previous year, in the depths of the Great Recession, to serve as the speech writer to the chairman and CEO. It had all sounded great at the time. The public affairs director had been completely enamored with my Harvard pedigree and was certain the CEO would be, too. Terrific.

I was excited because people I'd known who had been speech writers for admirals and generals had been privileged members of the inner circle. They'd enjoyed frequent, direct access to the boss and had all kinds of great things happen to their careers after leaving the job. It was one of those positions of special trust that opened all kinds of interesting doors, reserved only for those who'd breathed the rarefied air of the executive office. The same had to be true of someone writing speeches for a corporate CEO, right?

Wrong. My first day on the job, I learned I wasn't *the* speech writer, but *a* speech writer. Some twenty-something communications major was writing for the chairman, and I was to be her backup. I'd been duped. Nevertheless, with the economy crumbling and mass layoffs happening everywhere, I had to be content just to have a job. And that job consisted chiefly of writing employee newsletters and articles for the company intranet. I never even met the CEO.

Boredom quickly set in. While my central challenge on active duty had been to figure out how to cram hundreds of hours of work into something that vaguely resembled a normal work week, here, my challenge was to figure out how to take five hours of work and inflate it to fill a forty-hour week. It was vitally important that I do so, because I absolutely did *not* want to be perceived as an employee with excess capacity. All kinds of bad things happened to such people. They were loaded down with menial tasks. They were susceptible to assignment to every special project that came through the door. Some simply had their positions eliminated and were fired.

It was miserable. When orders came through to mobilize and deploy to Kuwait, I'm certain I would have swum there, just to get the hell out of corporate public affairs. And I had absolutely no desire to return there, ever. However, despite all the Skype interviewing and email networking I could manage from my cinder-block room at Kuwait Naval Base, I was unable to line up a new gig during my year in the desert. As the deployment wound down, I had to face the most depressing of all possible outcomes, a return to corporate public affairs. It was easily the most profound professional failure I had experienced to that point in my life.

The backup speech writer role was considered essential and had been filled by someone as soon as I'd left. Fine with me. I'd had more than my fill of backup speech writing. Upon my return, I was told my new role would be that of media advisor. I was to join the media group, whose job it was to prepare executives to talk to reporters. If those executives did not desire to interact with the media, my colleagues and I would do so on their behalf. There was nothing in my background to suggest I was qualified to do any of this, but it sounded mildly interesting. For a moment, I was hopeful.

Then I found out what my real job was. My new boss, Lauren, the media director, had been tasked to oversee construction of the company's long-planned visitor center. Rather than have an engineer or someone more suitably qualified manage the project, it was thought someone from corporate public affairs should. Lauren would be required to track the activities of various contractors and subcontractors and make progress reports to the CEO. As such, she'd convinced the public affairs director she needed a personal assistant to manage deadlines and to-do lists and schedule all of her meetings. I was to be that personal assistant.

I did not take the news well. While I had readily taken on countless tasks throughout my Navy career that were arguably beneath me, I had done so with a clear sense of purpose and out of loyalty to the service. None of that was present here. I felt not a twinge of loyalty to this organization, nor to the people in it, and I'd be damned if I was going to be some low-level corporate manager's personal assistant.

But I had no choice. I grumbled through the first few weeks, doing exactly as I was told. I'm sure it was obvious to everyone in the department that I was not pleased with my new duties, but I soldiered on.

Then, one day Lauren came back completely irate from a meeting I'd scheduled. The purpose of the meeting had been for her to strategize on ways to incorporate sustainability messages into the visitor center with the group of hippies the company had hired to contemplate such things. I had set up the meeting, as instructed, but hadn't set any agenda. I had no idea I was supposed to. Thus, both my boss and the hippies, thinking the other was going to lead the discussion, wound up having nothing to discuss. Everyone sat around awkwardly looking at each other before deciding to reschedule the meeting. Lauren had been embarrassed and it was apparently all my fault.

I found the whole thing hilarious. Lauren did not. She started chewing me out, which I absolutely did not appreciate. With my blood pressure rising, I waited until she'd finished and then told her, "You know what? You can schedule your own damn meetings from now on."

Her eyes went wide. After a brief pause, she chewed me out some more, telling me how many people in public affairs would kill to have my job and how grateful I should be to work for her. Then she shuffled off to her office.

The next day, I got called into Lauren's boss's office. I assumed I'd been summoned over the previous day's incident, and my intent was to explain it as a simple misunderstanding and then apologize profusely. It was quickly confirmed I had indeed been called in for that reason, but the conversation then took an unexpected turn.

"You know, Dan, you've been unusually irritable since you got back. You seem angry all the time. Lots of people have noticed."

Yup. Fair enough. I couldn't argue with that.

She continued, "I talked it over with Bob, and we think it would be best if you saw Dr. Harvey." Bob was the director of corporate public affairs, head of the entire department. Dr. Harvey was the staff psychologist.

"Something happened while you were deployed. It's none of my business, but you just don't seem yourself. I need you to see Dr. Harvey." It became clear that me seeing the shrink was more than a friendly suggestion. It was an order.

I couldn't decide if I was more insulted or amused. *You want me to see the shrink? Fine, I'll see the shrink.* I figured it couldn't be any worse than scheduling meetings and getting yelled at by Lauren.

Later that day, I wandered down to Dr. Harvey's office. It was conveniently located on the same floor as public affairs, right next to the corporate medical office. I wasn't sure why a large corporation required the full-time service of a psychologist, and I was curious as to how he spent his day. I never noticed anyone going in or coming out of his office. Maybe he read the newspapers and stared out the window to pass the time just like I did.

I knocked on Dr. Harvey's door and asked if I might have a brief word. I wasn't sure if I was supposed to make an appointment or launch directly into the so-called healing right then and there. Upon introducing myself, I noticed the beginnings of a smile creep across the corner of his mouth.

"Ah yes, Dan. I heard you might be stopping by." He was only a few years older than I, impeccably dressed, and, as far as I could judge, a good-looking guy.

"You did?" I asked.

"Yes. I understand you just returned from a deployment and may be having some trouble . . . readjusting." It was embarrassing to be having this conversation, but I appreciated his directness.

"Listen, Doc . . . It may be true I haven't exactly made a smooth transition back to life in corporate public affairs, but I'll guarantee you it has nothing to do with my deployment." This was privileged communication, so I figured I'd lay it all out for him.

"Well, your boss is convinced you're suffering from Post-Traumatic Stress Disorder."

I couldn't believe what I was hearing. To be clear, I had never been in combat. No one had ever shot at me. Aside from the general threats inherent to the region, I had been in absolutely zero danger while in Kuwait. I had spent every day of the deployment staring at screens in an air-conditioned trailer while sipping Starbucks and eating Pepperidge Farm Milano cookies. The very suggestion that I might be suffering from PTSD was beyond absurd.

Lauren didn't think so. She'd apparently watched some *60 Minutes* special on the struggles of combat veterans to reintegrate back into society and felt 100 percent confident in her diagnosis. As far as she was concerned, I exhibited all the symptoms.

I explained to Dr. Harvey that whatever stress I was experiencing was due entirely to the absurdity of my situation in corporate public affairs, not my Navy sabbatical. If anything, the sense of purpose and meaning I'd derived from a year on active duty served to fortify me against the forces of mediocrity that completely surrounded me in that corporate setting. Had it not been for that experience, I would likely have been far worse off. That said, a year in the desert had brought into sharp focus just how poor the quality of leadership was in the company, and I was not inclined to just shut up and accept it. In that sense, perhaps the deployment made my current situation worse. I could see both sides of it.

Dr. Harvey and I wound up having a terrific conversation. He was entirely sympathetic to my situation, but very rightly pointed out that further entanglements with my boss would likely get me fired. And no matter how great my boredom or frustration, neither would invite the pain and anxiety that unemployment would cause, particularly in a down economy. He said it was obvious that there was nothing wrong with me, but that I should stop in to vent whenever I felt the need. I could have done so every day but chose to limit subsequent visits to once per week. Dr. Harvey was a professional and a true gentleman, and I will always be grateful for my interaction with him.

Things eventually cooled down with Lauren. Not long after my initial discussion with the doctor, she felt compelled to offer me some words of encouragement.

"I know you've been seeing Dr. Harvey, Dan. And I want you to know I'm proud of you . . . for getting *help.*"

Thanks.

LESSONS LEARNED

1. Well intentioned employers often do more harm than good when attempting to get inside a veteran's head. At the same time, veterans often fail to appreciate that such interventions represent an employer's very generous alternative to simply firing their asses for behavior that would have gotten any other employee terminated.

2. More than 90 percent of Americans have never served in the military. As a result, many base their understanding of military men and women on Hollywood depictions of Navy SEALs. This contributes to a general ignorance of the military community that manifests itself in unusual, sometimes annoying ways. If you're a veteran, don't be surprised by this.

3. Instead, consider it an opportunity. Conduct yourself in such a manner as to reinforce positive perceptions civilians hold of members of the military. Have a personal code consistent with those values instilled through military service and live by it.

Some Day, You'll Be a Leader

"This lady sends a kid some cookies and suddenly she's Joshua Chamberlain at Little Round Top."

Corporate America, 2011.

I was trying to make it work with Lauren and the corporate media team.

There were four of us. Most impressive was Tom, our chief corporate spokesman. He'd been a local newscaster and was the envy of every corporate *communicator* within a five-state area. He got to hang out with the CEO, fly around on the corporate jet, talk to reporters from the *Wall Street Journal*, and make an occasional on-camera appearance. The rest of us were left to give soundbites to reporters from the local NPR affiliate at factory grand openings and write press releases. It was far from challenging work.

As media director, Lauren was at the zenith of her corporate career. This was evidenced by the fact she had four direct reports and an office instead of a cubicle. I didn't know Lauren well, but I knew one thing for certain: She didn't think much of me. Even after we got past her "diagnosis" of my supposed PTSD, I continued with my bad habit of telling her what little work she gave me was a complete waste of my time. Bosses tend not to appreciate such feedback.

One day, I got a call from my wife. She was at the doctor's office with our six-year-old daughter, who was fighting off what we thought was an upper respiratory infection. The doctor ran some tests and discovered our daughter had developed asthma, causing her difficulty in breathing. She went on to explain the combination of asthma and illness could cause our daughter to stop breathing in the middle of the night. Not good. The doctor thus directed that our daughter be admitted to the hospital for overnight observation.

My wife spent the night with our daughter in the hospital, and I went home. The next morning, I went to work, as usual, and walked past Lauren's office on my way to the cafeteria to get a cup of coffee. My plan was to put in a normal day's work and then catch up with my wife and daughter at the hospital that evening.

"Hey Dan . . ." Lauren was motioning me into her office.

Dammit, I thought. I hated going into that office, having to feign interest in whatever she had to say.

"Yes, ma'am? What can I do for you?" I put on my usual, fake smile.

"Isn't your daughter in the hospital?" she asked.

"Yes," I said, "but my wife is with her. She had a good night and is doing much better."

Thanks for asking. Now let me get my coffee.

"Well, don't hang around here," Lauren replied. "You should go to the hospital to be with your little girl."

Never one to disobey a lawful order, I promptly departed for the hospital. I found my way to my daughter's room where she was sitting up in bed, coloring, while my wife flipped through a magazine on an adjacent couch. Upon noticing me, my daughter pointed to the small table next to her bed and said, "Look what your work sent me, Daddy!"

On the table sat an enormous cookie bouquet. About a dozen, very large sugar cookies sat on sticks, arranged to look like a bundle of flowers. I noticed a card stuck between the stems. On it was written, "We hope you get well soon! Love, Your friends at . . ." The handwriting was unmistakably Lauren's.

I had to admit, I was touched. What an incredibly kind gesture. I had no idea how Lauren had even found out my daughter was sick, but anyone who could put a smile on her face while in the hospital had my gratitude. Maybe I'd misjudged Lauren. We all have our shortcomings. Maybe she deserved to be forgiven for hers. And maybe I owed it to her to be a decent employee for a change.

The next morning, I went straight to Lauren's office. I wanted her to know just how grateful I was that she'd brightened my kid's day. And even though I'd never say the words, I wanted to somehow communicate to Lauren that I'd resolved to be better. I wasn't entirely sure how, given how little I had to do, but I would figure it out. I would write the best damn press releases she'd ever seen. Things were going to be different.

"Lauren, may I interrupt you?" Good opening, I thought. Show her a little deference. That will set the right tone.

"Sure, Dan. Come on in." Lauren was at her desk, scribbling notes in a day planner.

"Lauren, I want to thank you very sincerely for the cookie bouquet you sent my daughter. She loved it. It was the first thing she showed me when I got to the hospital yesterday. And she wanted you to have this."

I presented Lauren the finger-painted thank-you card my daughter had made in the pediatric ward's craft room.

"Oh, how cute," she said, examining the misshapen ponies my kid had drawn. "It was no trouble at all."

"No, really, Lauren . . . you put a big smile on her face. My wife and I were grateful for that. Thank you." For once, I was being sincere.

Lauren looked up from the card and gazed at me for a moment. Her expression suggested she was mulling something deep and profound.

"Well, Dan . . . Someday, *you'll* be a leader. You'll remember this, and you'll know how to take care of your people."

I felt my face go flush. *Excuse me? Someday, I'll be a leader? Someday? Was she being serious?*

Apparently, yes. The look on her face made obvious her tremendous pride in having just taught me an invaluable life lesson.

Lauren's comment illustrated perfectly the chasm that existed between us. She had no idea who I was, where I'd been, or what I was capable of doing. I'd had nearly two decades of experience leading men and women in the United States Navy and had been responsible for more people and hard assets by the time I was 25 than Lauren would in three lifetimes.

Yet, *she* was going to lecture *me* on leadership? This lady sends a kid some cookies and suddenly she's Joshua Chamberlain at Little Round Top.

"Uh . . . right. Well, thanks again." I turned and got the hell out of there.

Our relationship promptly turned south. I simply could not take Lauren seriously, about leadership or anything else. Ultimately, I left the group, with her help. She wanted me gone just as badly as I wanted to leave. Lauren wrote the recommendation letters that led to the promotion that moved me out of her group.

I'd heard that one way to get rid of a poorly performing employee was to promote him, but I never believed it until it happened to me.

LESSONS LEARNED

1. Many employers take great pride in hanging the *We Hire Veterans* sign in the window. But that doesn't mean its leaders have any understanding whatsoever of a veteran's

unique experiences or capabilities. Veterans should have no expectation they will.

2. Laurens are common. If you're a veteran, you'd better think twice before you attempt to "fix" one by educating her on your military achievements. She'll find it condescending and things will get worse. Trust me.

3. Laurens wait their entire careers to have a single subordinate to lead, and there's no way in hell they're going to let you ruin the experience. So let them have it. If you can't stomach being that subordinate, go somewhere else.

Money Talks

"Sorry, Captain. I'm not on watch."

Aboard USS Ponce, *North Arabian Gulf, 2013.*

I t was glorious to be underway again.

When presented an opportunity to take a sabbatical from the *corporate clown show* to serve as the air boss on *USS Ponce*, I jumped at it. Goodbye, pretend-like-I-give-a-shit drudgery. Hello, flight suits, salt air, and cigars under the stars! And because it was to be a brief, ninety-day respite, courtesy of the US Navy Reserve, I intended to relish every second of it.

And relish it I did. Even the slightest detail that would have otherwise escaped my attention while I was on active duty brought me the most terrific pleasure. Whenever I opened a hatch to step inside the skin of the ship, I savored that pungent, metal-diesel-hamburger-grease smell that immediately smacked you in the face—that stench known by every sailor that clung to your clothes as though it possessed you. *Such an exquisite bouquet!* And that freezing burst of cold air that shot directly on the back of your bare neck from one of the ducts in the overly air-conditioned combat information center? *Heaven!* The burnt-popcorn taste of the twelve-hour-old sludge that passed as coffee on the bridge? *Sublime!* Yes, I savored every bit of it.

Meals in the wardroom were especially enjoyable. You never knew who you might strike up a conversation with, given *Ponce's* ever-rotating cast of characters. Then in her fifth decade of service, she'd recently transitioned from an amphibious transport ship to a special mission platform, drawing special operators and members of various three-lettered agencies from around the world. Acting as host was a mixed crew of 200 civilian mariners of the US Military Sealift Command, or MSC; forty active duty US Navy sailors; and one Navy reserve aviator to serve as the air boss, or director of flight operations. A Navy captain was in overall command, assisted by an MSC captain with responsibility for all civilian mariners. It was far and away the motliest crew with which I'd ever sailed. I was all but guaranteed a fascinating, even enlightening, experience every time I stepped foot in the wardroom.

Such was the case on a random Tuesday afternoon while pier side in Bahrain. I was enjoying a corn dog and baked beans with my good friend, Rob, an MSC third mate and recent graduate of the US Merchant Marine Academy at King's Point. Rob was an interesting cat. He'd been home-schooled, was extraordinarily well read, well-traveled, thoroughly engaging in conversation, and smart as all hell. He was the kind of guy who took the time to actually read the technical manual for whatever new gadget found its way to the bridge and enjoyed doing so. Rob was the perfect companion in any port, having studied the appropriate guidebooks for a given location well in advance. He knew the local customs and fare, all the right bars and restaurants to seek out, and, importantly, which among them were known for the best cigar selections. He was a frequent visitor to the ship's control tower during flight operations, where, between aircraft launches and recoveries, we would debrief previous port visits and identify any lessons-learned we could apply to strategies for future ones. I greatly admired Rob for his unwavering commitment to employ his insatiable curiosity, superior intellect, and high energy in useful endeavors—chiefly, martini-drinking and cigar-smoking. He was my kind of guy.

Rob had just finished a shift as the deck watch officer. Relieved of his official duties, we quickly became engrossed in a conversation on the various subtleties and clever innuendos of the *Archer* episode we'd watched the night before. We carried on for several minutes until, from the table next to us, the MSC captain interrupted.

"Hey, Rob . . . we just found out we're getting underway at zero-nine-hundred tomorrow morning. Could you update the sailing board?"

The sailing board was an MSC thing. It was a simple chalkboard, mounted on an easel, and placed in a conspicuous position on the ship's quarterdeck whenever in port. It contained information essential to all MSC personnel: which duty section was on watch, the time of sunset and sunrise, when the ship was next getting underway, etc. I'd never seen such a thing in the Navy. Still, I had to admit, it was a simple, low-tech, highly effective communication tool. Some sailors, inclined to indulge in the myriad distractions available in port, confined their knowledge of shipboard activities only to what was written on the sailing board. I could fully appreciate why the captain wanted to keep it current.

Rob, ever the proper and attentive watch officer, promptly responded with, "Sorry, Captain. I'm not on watch."

Not on watch? I thought I was hearing things. No, he couldn't have said that. I waited for Rob to follow up with a quick, "Just kidding, sir."

But he didn't. The words just hung there. Not on watch? Who gives a shit whether you're on watch? When the captain asks you to do something, you frickin' do it! Rob knew that, didn't he? He was a professional. He was one of the smartest guys I knew. And he was my friend. But none of that mattered if he was stupid enough to slough off a request from his captain with his lame-ass "I'm not on watch."

My Navy brain could hardly process what had just happened. On a warship, the captain's authority is absolute. He shoulders the *mantle of command*, and in so doing, is rightly owed the respect and obedience of all hands. The Navy selects officers for such positions with the utmost care. Captains were highly seasoned, well-rounded professionals who, through decades of service, had demonstrated the highest integrity, soundest judgement, and greatest proficiency in sailing and fighting ships at sea. Anything that happened anywhere on that ship or in the waters surrounding it was *entirely* his responsibility.

Not on watch? Bullshit! If *my* captain asked *me* to update the damn sailing board, I couldn't drop my corn dog fast enough to do it.

Instinctively, I leaned back in my chair, away from Rob. I didn't know exactly how the captain was going to respond, but I certainly did not want to be in the line of fire. I half expected to hear the dull "thwump" of a .50 caliber round hitting a cantaloupe, whereupon Rob's head would explode.

Well, my friend, there's nothing I can do for you now, I thought. *You bring that weak, I'm-not-on-watch bullshit, and I'm afraid you're on your own.*

Then something truly bizarre happened. Rather than split Rob's skull with invective, the captain instead replied, "Okay. Who came on watch after you?"

"The navigator."

"All right. I'll ask him."

The matter thus settled, the captain went back to work on his Boston cream pie, and Rob turned back to me and asked, "Where were we? Oh, yeah . . . I love it when he threatens to make Millhouse eat the bowl of cobwebs. Freaking hilarious!" He'd shifted back to *Archer* as though the exchange with the captain had never even taken place.

I was flummoxed. *What the hell had just happened?*

Later that night, Rob and I were sitting in the tower waiting for a flight of Navy Seahawk helicopters to arrive. The aircraft were still a ways out, so we had some time to kill. I thus took the opportunity to press Rob for an explanation as to what had happened with the captain at lunch.

He began by explaining that all civilian mariners are paid by the hour, from able seaman to captain. As such, whether one was *on the clock* determined whether one was paid. By contrast, all members of the US military are salaried employees. From seaman recruit to admiral, Navy sailors are *always* on the clock. Civilian mariners are also entitled to overtime pay whenever they are required to perform work-related tasks outside their prescribed work hours. Such pay can run to two or three times a mariner's regular hourly rate if the work is performed both outside normal hours and during certain *protected* times of day. These included breaks and mealtimes.

I told Rob I knew nothing of MSC's pay policy and assumed I'd witnessed an act of gross insubordination. Not so, he said. What actually took place was an unspoken conversation that went something like this:

Captain: "Hey, Rob. I'm pretty sure you're on watch right now. Could you go update the sailing board?"

Rob: "Actually, Captain, I've been relieved and am no longer on watch. Of course, I'd be more than happy to update the sailing board for you. But, as you know, I would then be entitled to both an hour of overtime, as well as an hour of penalty pay, because it's lunch time. You would thus incur a cost three times that of my normal rate if I were to perform this task for you. Given that, I want to extend the courtesy of informing you that I am not, in fact, currently on the clock."

Captain: "Oh. Well, thank you for that, Rob. If I simply ask the current watchstander to update the sailing board, I would incur none of the additional costs you described. So, please tell me if you would, who is currently on watch?"

Rob: "The navigator."

Captain: "Very well. I'll ask him to do it. Thank you again, Rob. Please carry on with your corn dog and enjoy the rest of your day."

Rob: "Thank you, Captain. You do the same."

Well, I'll be damned, I thought. I'd completely misread the situation. But who could blame me? I'd been taught to regard captains with fear and awe since I was seventeen years old. Rob had not been so raised. To him, and all the other civilian mariners, one's relationship with the captain was purely business. It was a very grown-up arrangement.

LESSONS LEARNED

1. The average employee doesn't leap at the opportunity to do additional work for which they will not be paid. That's rational. And the average employer doesn't willingly incur additional cost via overtime and penalty pay when they don't have to. That, too, is rational.

2. What may be perceived as an act of insubordination might actually be an act of great loyalty. Get the facts before you pass judgement.

3. I didn't fully appreciate the role money did *not* play in my Navy experience until I left. It was seldom the reason I did or did not do any particular thing. That was a terrific way to live.

MISADVENTURE NO. 11

Be Consistent

"I don't go looking for trash."

Aboard USS Fletcher, *North Arabian Gulf, 2002.*

C ritical to one's development as an effective human being is to *know thyself.* And one of the many things I know about myself is that I don't enjoy working while drunk, standing at a urinal, at two o'clock in the morning. I know this because I had a boss who required I do exactly that.

We'd been underway, operating around-the-clock, for fifty straight days. I'm sure it had been fifty days, because we'd had a Beer Day. Beer Days, in which every member of the crew was issued exactly two beers, only happened after a ship had been at sea for forty-five continuous days. It was a tough way to enjoy a couple of beers—but, without fail, they were the most delicious you'd ever tasted. For the rest of my life, I'll remember with great fondness every beer I ever consumed on Beer Day.

My buddies and I bolted for the officers' club the second the ship tied to the pier in Bahrain. Late 2002 was a very active time in the North Arabian Gulf, so the club was packed. Familiar faces were everywhere—Naval Academy classmates, friends from flight school—and everyone was having a great time, which carried on right up until curfew. Just as your parents did when you were in high school, the Navy required that you be home at a certain time. And there was always someone waiting up, ready to ground you if you were late. So, as was usually the case, my fellow lieutenants and I ended the evening with a sprint down the pier to get back aboard the ship at the last possible moment. We made it. Barely.

Safely across the finish line, I headed straight to the head (Navy-speak for bathroom) to take care of business before stumbling to my stateroom to collapse onto my rack. I was feeling more than a little out of it standing at the urinal, thoroughly polluted by too much booze and cigar smoke, when I noticed the shape of a person appear beside me.

"Dan . . . glad I finally found you. There's a problem with the AMRR." It was my boss, Lieutenant Commander Wright.

The AMRR, or Aircraft Material Readiness Report, was my nightly pain in the ass. It was an overly complicated and detailed report that kept the squadron, air wing, battle group, Pentagon, White House, Buckingham Palace, and the Vatican all apprised of our detachment's readiness to meet mission requirements. As the maintenance officer, it was my job to ensure it was completed and sent every night.

"See here? It still says Six Three is NMC for that AFCS problem. I thought the guys fixed that right before we pulled in." In other words, aircraft Six Three was annotated as not mission capable for a problem with its automatic flight control system.

He was correct. The repair had been made, and the aircraft was back to fully mission capable status. But so what? It was just a damn report, and it was two o'clock in the morning. Couldn't we just fix it in the next night's report?

"We'll need to send out a corrected report ASAP." *Shit.*

Now, some may applaud this. *He's holding you to a high standard. Bravo!* But the trouble with Lieutenant Commander Wright was, everything had to be perfect, all the time. And when everything had to be perfect, nothing usually was. Things got half-assed, because people knew from the outset they would have to be done over and over again until the boss's impossibly high standard was met. There was no such thing as "do it right the first time," because there never was only a first time. That's a very dangerous dynamic for an organization, because not only does it waste time, but also, when everything is deemed the *most important thing*, you risk losing sight of those few things that truly are.

So, sure enough, Lieutenant Commander Wright followed me back to my stateroom where, as he looked over my shoulder, I fired up my computer and spent the next hour writing and rewriting the *entire* AMRR. You see, it wasn't good enough just to correct the error concerning aircraft Six Three. No, he thought it better to recheck all the numbers and provide some additional commentary. By the end, I'd fully transitioned from drunk to hungover.

The next day at lunch, my fellow aviators could hardly contain themselves as I recounted the two o'clock urinal conversation and the AMRR rewrite that followed. To have a laugh at someone else's expense was pure gold on deployment, and my misfortune was received as a wonderful gift.

When the laughter died down and we returned our attention to our sliders, my buddy concluded the conversation by saying, "Wright . . . what a clown. So typical!" Everyone shook his head in agreement and repeated, "So typical."

In the final analysis, Lieutenant Commander Wright was a micromanaging, shitty boss. But he was as consistent as the sunrise in his micromanaging shittiness. And that, in a strange way, made him far easier to tolerate and manage. Yes, it frustrated me most days. But I didn't have to devote an ounce of mental energy to anticipating Wright's next move. If there were any way to over-complicate a situation and piss off anyone having anything to do with it, he would. Knowing this, I could often get out ahead of him and minimize the damage.

If consistency can partially offset the negative qualities of a poor leader, imagine how it might amplify and make more accessible the positive tendencies of a good one.

Aboard USS Ponce, *North Arabian Gulf, 2013.*

A decade removed from writing AMRRs, I found myself suddenly promoted to executive officer, or second-in-command, of *USS Ponce*. This promotion surprised everyone, including me, because I had what I thought were two disqualifying features: I was an aviator, and I was a reservist. As a pilot, I'd spent almost all my time at sea flying off the back of ships, not driving them. And as a reservist, I'd had significant gaps in my operational experience. The Navy was a part-time gig, and it had been a full decade since I'd spent any significant time underway.

But this was a non-traditional ship led by a non-traditional captain, a harmonica-playing, former door-to-door Bible salesman.

The captain and I hit it off immediately. I'd been ordered to the ship as the air boss and was drawn by his unconventional style. Once I'd settled into the role and demonstrated I could safely and efficiently move aircraft on and off the flight deck, the captain allowed me free reign. At one point, I called him on the bridge in the middle of flight operations to inform him of some non-standard rearranging of air traffic I intended to do to manage a busier-than-usual flight schedule.

"You don't need to call me," he said. "I trust you. Just do what you need to do."

About the time I was beginning to feel comfortable as air boss, I was promoted to executive officer, a role for which even I questioned my suitability. But if that's what the captain wanted, then I would throw myself into it and give him my very best.

Not knowing exactly where to start, I decided to focus on the Plan of the Day. On most Navy ships, the executive officer, or XO, owns this document, which serves as the ship's daily schedule and sets the working rhythm of the crew. It's the XO's responsibility to ensure that day-to-day activities prescribed by the plan are properly sequenced, coordinated, and resourced so the ship can meet its mission requirements.

Step one was to write the plan, which I usually did after dinner with the help of the operations officer. Step two was to oversee its smooth execution, which required that I run all over the ship most of the following day. I worked out early most mornings, before the day's activities commenced, to ensure I didn't lose the habit to fatigue or unexpected events.

About one week into my tenure as XO, I wandered up to the combat information center, know as Combat, after my workout to check in with the operations officer. He had the early morning shift as the watch officer in Combat, and he was the first person I sought each morning to find out if anything unusual had happened overnight. Most nights, the ship would benignly steam in its assigned box, leaving nothing for the operations officer and me to discuss in the morning. But this morning, I could tell immediately upon entering that something was amiss.

"Captain was here about half an hour ago, and he was *piiisssed . . .*"

Uh-oh. The captain was a pretty easy-going guy who didn't rile frequently. As with me, he afforded most members of the crew a long leash and stayed focused on results, just as a good boss should. But it would have been a mistake to have interpreted his laid-back style as permitting of sloppiness when it came to matters of safety or the smooth, by-the-book execution of shipboard evolutions. When it came to those things, the captain could be a tyrant.

We'd been scheduled to launch small boats from the well deck at 6:00 a.m. This was an interesting evolution, in which sea water stored in huge ballast tanks was pumped to the ass end of the ship, sinking a portion of the stern and flooding the Olympic pool-sized space under the flight deck that held the small boats. Once flooded, the boats would cast off lines and motor off. It was pretty cool to watch. And watch was all I usually did as air boss, because I had nothing to contribute to the safe conduct of small-boat launches. If anything, I would have gotten in the way.

I assumed the same was true now that I was the XO, so I'd remained in the gym that morning while the boats launched. And about the time I was knocking out my last set of squats, the captain had wandered into Combat to ensure everything was in place throughout the ship for a safe, successful evolution. It was then he'd discovered we were out of position. Rather than be at our appointed launch point, the ship was instead still in its night steaming box, some twenty miles away. The captain immediately canceled the boat launch, ordered the well deck to be drained, and set course for the correct launch point. And then he removed several layers of skin from the operations officer's ass.

There had apparently been some miscommunication that had caused the screw-up. This was of little consolation to the operations officer, who was an otherwise capable, conscientious, and highly professional officer. All he could say to me was, "You should have been here, man . . . you should have been here."

As I thought about it, I realized he was exactly right. I *should* have been there. I owned the Plan of the Day, and the boat launch was a significant event on that day's plan. I don't know what, exactly, I could or should have done to ensure the ship was in the proper position, but I certainly could have been in Combat when the captain had arrived to take my rightful portion of the ass-chewing. I resolved then and there to be on the scene well prior to the commencement of any significant evolution to assess for myself whether its participants had crossed all the t's and dotted all the i's to ensure a successful event. I knew I wouldn't know all the right questions to ask every time, but I thought I could at least cover the most basic, obvious stuff. And I also figured I'd get better at asking the right questions as time went on.

This became my new routine. We were scheduled to launch boats again the next morning, so I stopped by Combat about an hour before launch time. The operations officer smirked when I walked in and said, "I figured you'd be here." Not much else needed to be said, so I continued to the well deck, where preparations were underway to flood the deck and launch the boats.

I walked up to the boatswain's mate in charge of the evolution and asked, "Hey, Chief . . . any reason we shouldn't get the boats off on time this morning?" He replied, "No, sir." Satisfied we were reasonably set for success, I lingered a while longer to chat with members of the boat crews and drink my coffee. A few minutes later, the captain appeared.

"Any reason we shouldn't get the boats off on time this morning, Chief?"

"No, sir," the chief replied. And then the captain departed for the bridge.

Hmm. Maybe I was onto something.

The pattern repeated itself throughout the day. About fifteen minutes before any major evolution, the captain would arrive on the scene, ask a few simple questions, and then, if satisfied with the answers, promptly depart. Always fifteen minutes. Always the same questions. I thus made it my practice to arrive thirty minutes before any event, ask the same questions I thought the captain would ask, and then hang around until the boss arrived to see how close I'd gotten.

In working to refine and improve my approach to managing the Plan of the Day, I discovered the captain kept a very regular routine. That was interesting to me, because, aboard a ship, the captain answers to no one. He does what he wants, when he wants to do it. Why bother with a routine? No one knows how exactly the captain spends his time, only that he always seems to know what's going on everywhere, all the time, often without leaving his chair on the bridge. Yes, various watchstanders brought him regular reports on various happenings throughout the course of the day, but that alone wouldn't fully explain how good captains seemed omniscient.

The discovery of the captain's routine provided a powerful insight on how I could be more effective in my role. My ultimate goal as XO was not merely to avoid the captain's wrath, nor to prevent others from avoiding the same. Rather, I wanted to learn how to effectively run a warship at sea. It was highly unlikely I'd ever be captain. After all, I had little business even being an executive officer. But I thought there were numerous leadership lessons to be learned that I could apply in numerous other settings. Being a good XO would one day help me to be a good boss. With that in mind, I continued to observe the captain closely.

Given his experience, the captain instinctively knew what *right* looked like in any given situation. He could quickly assess whether all proper procedures had been followed and necessary precautions had been taken to ensure success. It was pattern recognition. As soon as he was satisfied that all the pieces were in their proper place, he moved on. Or, if they weren't, he promptly took corrective action.

Later, I made another useful discovery. I was standing on the bridge next to the captain, admiring a spectacular Arabian Gulf sunset, when he remarked, "There's a good bit of trash piling up outside Repair Three. Why don't you see if you can do something about that?"

Trash? Repair Three? I knew Repair Three was one of the ship's many repair lockers (closets that contained firefighting and damage control gear), but I had no idea where it was. So, the first order of business was to find it. Being the typical male, I refused to ask anyone for directions, certain I could find it myself. A half hour later, having wandered fore and aft, up and down, and in and out of various hatches, I was no closer to finding Repair Three than when I'd first left the bridge. Defeated, I finally asked a passing sailor, "Could you kindly point me in the direction of Repair Three?"

A short time later, I was standing in front of the repair locker where, sure enough, there lay a pile of trash. I stuck my head through the hatch of the adjoining space and asked its occupants, "You guys know anything about the trash piled up out here?"

"Yes, sir. I suppose we've just lacked the ambition to drag it all the way to the incinerator the last couple of days." Sailors . . . they're so refreshingly, unapologetically honest.

"Well, gents, this being a US Navy warship and all, we probably shouldn't let the trash pile up here or anywhere else. Pretty sure I read that in Navy Regulations. Do me a favor, and see if you can muster the energy to take the trash out *every* day, capisce?"

"Got it, sir. No problem."

There was absolutely nothing remarkable about this exchange. Since the earliest days of sail, officers have had to remind sailors to take out the trash. What *was* remarkable, at least to me, was how the captain knew there was trash piling up in some obscure corner of the ship in the first place. Didn't he have more important things to do than patrol the passageways for garbage?

I decided to ask.

"I don't necessarily go looking for trash," he explained. "I just want to know what's happening aboard the ship. And I want to see for myself that we're maintaining an acceptable state of good order and discipline. The clues are everywhere, if you look for them. Cleanliness is one. So, I walk the entire ship, every day, same route, usually at about the same time. Most days, I do it twice, once in the morning and again in the evening."

Fascinating. What else?

"The best part is, I get to enjoy chance encounters with sailors in their own environments. I get to learn about them and understand their experiences. It's good for them to see the captain out and about, every day, interested in what they're doing. And they often provide me some very useful perspective. It's a good thing for me to see the ship through their eyes."

The captain estimated he spent no more than forty-five minutes a day walking the ship and considered it an invaluable investment of his time. It was an established part of his routine that yielded considerable benefits, both for him and the crew. Those encounters enabled him to connect with sailors in an informal, yet meaningful way, and helped him maintain a highly accurate, almost intuitive sense of the health of the organization he led. And, let's be honest, those walks kept the crew on its toes. When people knew the captain was out and about, they tended to put a little more sparkle in their daily tasks.

Consistency. Predictability. These are good-boss traits that can be easily cultivated. I decided to try for myself. "Mind if I tag along on your next walk, Captain?"

"Not at all. I'll teach you my route."

So, in addition to arriving on the scene thirty minutes prior to any significant evolution, I made a routine of walking the ship. I wasn't trying to *be* the captain; rather, I was trying to develop a similar level of awareness of what was happening aboard as that which the Captain so easily maintained. In doing so, I hoped to get ahead of problems that, ultimately, would never even come to the captain's attention. That was good for him and the crew. A pile of trash outside Repair Three? Never again!

After several weeks of keeping my new routine, I felt I'd fallen into a steadier, more productive, more enjoyable rhythm. It's a good feeling to move through the day with purpose, and no one seemed particularly surprised by or annoyed with the micro-incursions I made on their day. After all, the XO was supposed to get into people's business from time to time. It was in the job description. But I felt I was doing so in predictable ways and for legitimate reasons. I felt I was creating value, not thoughtlessly destroying it.

Near the end of my tenure, I experienced what I considered my capstone event. It came early in what was scheduled to be a busy, busy day. We had a contingent of special operators aboard doing a variety of sneaky things in the small boats launched from our well deck, as well as a detachment of Army Apache helicopters, doing some proof-of-concept work that would (or would not) demonstrate that the Army and Navy could play together in this rather unique operating environment.

The operations officer and I had worked hard on the day's choreography, scheduling events down to five-minute increments. Of course, the plan almost never played out exactly as written, but we'd baked in time for various contingencies, thoroughly pre-briefed all the players, and knew our seasoned crew would act with smooth efficiency when the curtain went up. It was indeed a tough schedule, but by no means an impossible one.

Despite the early hour, I'd already made my usual rounds. I'd checked in with the boat crews, with the guys on the flight deck, and with the operations officer in Combat. At every stop, I'd found people well prepared, focused, and completely on task. Thus satisfied, I made my way to the bridge and positioned myself next to the captain's chair.

The captain's chair, and the area surrounding it, is a place of high honor on any warship, much as you might expect Darth Vader's setup to be on the bridge of any Star Destroyer. It consists of an elevated La-Z-Boy with the block letters "CO" embroidered on the back, surrounded by closed-circuit TV monitors, radios, and phones, from which the occupant can oversee events anywhere aboard the ship. The captain's chair is an important symbol of command and is sacrosanct. *No one* puts a butt cheek there, except the commanding officer. He, and he alone, owned that privilege.

As was always his habit, the captain arrived on the bridge and took his seat about ten minutes before the first scheduled boat launch. I had learned the captain's first few minutes on the bridge was not a time for idle chat-chat. He'd settle in, check the monitors, have a look at a few emails, drink half a cup of coffee, and then stare at the horizon. It all took about five minutes. Only then would he then glance around the bridge and notice, for the first time, anyone else who might be standing there.

My goal was to be the first person he noticed. I didn't crave the attention. Rather, I wanted to be immediately available should something be out of place or not to his liking. It would give the Captain an immediate resource with which to fix a problem while, at the same time, sparing others aboard from an unpleasant encounter with the boss first thing in the morning. Plus, it made me feel useful. While the jury was still out on whether I was any good at this XO thing, being the captain's go-to guy made me feel like I was at least trying.

I felt as ready as anyone could be to answer any question on any detail on any event on the entire Plan of the Day. *Bring it on, Captain!* But as he emerged from his morning ritual, the captain simply nodded a hello in my direction, returned his focus to the horizon, and asked me, with a tone of complete contentment, "Is there *any* place else you'd rather be right now?"

The boss was feeling good, and rightfully so. The crew was fully prepared for whatever the day might bring.

And in the end, they *nailed* it. The Plan went off without a hitch. It was *Swan Lake* in blue camouflage.

Is there any place else I'd rather be? Somewhere other than a warship at sea with a captain who enforces the highest standard of professionalism through total consistency of thought, word, and deed?

No, sir. Absolutely not.

LESSONS LEARNED

1. Employees are quick to pick up on a boss's tendencies and even quicker to notice when he departs from them. Consistency is a core, good-boss behavior.

2. When the boss consistently aligns their behavior and activities to a set of clear priorities and expectations, it's powerful. People can go about their business without having to worry about the boss's shifting whims or whether an activity that's acceptable today might get them in trouble tomorrow. That's liberating.

3. It's useful to have a routine. If you haven't done so already, develop one, and work to continuously refine and improve it. You'll be more effective. And your employees will thank you for it.

Go Get Your Shine Box

"No more shines, Billy . . .
I don't shine shoes anymore."

Aboard USS Ponce, *North Arabian Gulf, 2013.*

"XO, Captain here . . . Could you come see me on the bridge?"

It was one of my last mornings aboard *USS Ponce*, known as The Proud Lion, and one of the few remaining times my radio would ring with those words. The thought depressed me.

The captain had summoned me for a chat with our visiting commodore. Commodore, formerly an official rank in the US Navy, is an honorific given to the commander of a group of ships, aviation squadrons, SEAL teams, etc. Many such officers regularly moved in and out of the Persian Gulf operating area, and the captain had extended an open invitation to any who wished to set up shop in *Ponce* with his staff for as long as he wanted. Given all the tricked-out gear we had aboard, it was a pretty compelling offer.

The commodore was scheduled to visit two of his nearby destroyers that morning. When the time of his departure arrived, the captain asked me to escort him down to the well deck. For one not familiar with the ship, the route could be a bit confusing, and the captain intended to spare his VIP guest any such confusion. I would therefore serve as his personal guide.

And I was happy to do it. By that point in my tour, I'd come to know the ship quite well. As we traversed the passageways and ladders leading to the well deck, I gave the commodore the abbreviated version of my usual tour, sharing factoids, bits of *Ponce* history, and points of interest along the way. I'd done the same for twenty or so previous visitors and had enjoyed it tremendously each time. You really learn to appreciate a place when you get to play tour guide.

We pushed through the final hatch to the half-flooded well deck where the commodore's boat and crew were standing by. I walked him around the perimeter of the space to the catwalk that led to the access ladder from which he could make his way down to the boat. Once there, he deftly swung himself on to the ladder and began descending, but suddenly stopped about halfway down.

The commodore looked up at me. "Don't take this the wrong way, XO, but you're having *way* too much fun here." He gave me a half smile, then descended the remaining rungs of the latter, boarded the boat, and shoved off.

Too much fun?

I headed back to the bridge to share the commodore's comment with the captain. He found it hilarious.

"He's right, dammit! You *are* having too much fun here. I should probably do something about that." We both had a laugh and then got on with the day.

But the comment stuck with me. Later that night, after I had finished briefing the captain on a schedule issue, I asked, "Does the commodore think I'm delusional? Am I *Ponce's* village idiot or something?"

No, no, no, the captain assured me. The commodore had actually commented on how professionally he thought I conducted myself and that I was held in high regard among members of his staff. He was just busting my balls a little, the captain insisted. "Don't read anything into it."

To be fair, my disposition was unnaturally sunny for a person on extended deployment to the Middle East. But who could blame me? I was having an absolute blast, and I didn't want it to end. I was in my natural environment, surrounded by my people—my tribe—doing interesting, important stuff every waking minute of the day. Those who encountered me enjoyed the very best version of myself I could offer. Engaged. Attentive. Informed. Energetic. Eager-to-serve. Like Tony Robbins, the motivational speaker, I went to bed every night "exhausted and victorious." I was everything I had never been as a civilian. It didn't get any better.

And because people experienced me at my very best, opportunities poured in from every direction. The captain asked me to extend aboard through the end of his tour, an additional six months. The senior officer in charge of one of the exercises we'd hosted offered me a position on his staff. The officer who'd first brought me to *Ponce* as air boss asked me to stick around. In the weird, special operations, Afloat Forward Staging Base world, I was a pretty popular guy.

It was hugely tempting to take one of the offers, remain in uniform a while longer, and kick the civilian can down the road. Returning to the cubicle after such an experience would be one of the hardest things I'd ever have to do. But I knew I eventually would. I couldn't avoid it. While I'd found tremendous success and satisfaction in *Ponce*, it was not a path back to a full-time Navy career. It didn't work that way. Once you quit active duty, even if you continued in the reserves, the service moved on without you. No one was irreplaceable.

Besides, avoiding the civilian world was chicken shit. I'd had a pretty miserable experience, but I wasn't about to give up. I'd made a significant investment in a private-sector career, and I intended to realize a return on that investment. And I absolutely refused to be defeated by the likes of Andrew and Lauren. *No frickin' way.* One way or another, I was determined to find the same success as a civilian as I'd found as a US Naval officer.

Corporate America, 2013.

I thus returned to my marketing job with a chip on my shoulder. I'd successfully exited corporate public affairs the year prior to take a marketing job with the same company. In doing so, I thought I had improved my career situation, but just barely. Marketing, in the role I then occupied, had far more to do with tradeshows and newsletters than it did with the fundamentals I'd been taught in business school: product, place, promotion, and price. When I'd made the move, I'd hoped I would finally get my hands on at least a few of the levers that drove business outcomes. Not so, it turned out. Despite the ambiguous, made-up title my boss had given me, strategic marketing consultant, he was content to have me write communication plans for product launches. No need to bother myself with segmentation analyses or pricing strategies that drove earnings. Someone in corporate did that stuff.

Every time he brought me another communication plan to write, I felt like Tommy, Joe Pesci's character in *Goodfellas*.

Billy (old-time mobster): "Now this kid, this kid was great. They used to call him Spit Shine Tommy."

Tommy: "No more shines, Billy . . . I don't shine shoes anymore."

Billy (later, antagonizing Tommy): "Now go home and get your fucking shine box!"

Tommy (smashing the glass from which he was drinking): "Motherfucking mutt! You big piece of shit!"

Later, Tommy bludgeons, stabs, and shoots Billy multiple times before dumping his body.

"Write a communication plan," was my, "Now go home and get your fucking shine box!"

But before he had me get my shine box, my boss asked me to debrief members of our team on my *Ponce* experience. "Tell people what you were up to out there," he said. "I'm sure they'd find it interesting."

Hell, no! was my initial response. That experience was mine and mine alone. No way was I sharing it with a bunch of corporate losers. They wouldn't understand, anyway. But then I reconsidered. Everyone knew me as Dan, the communications guy. Why not show them Lieutenant Commander Dan Bozung, air boss and executive officer? Maybe my colleagues, and my boss, would take me seriously for a change.

So I poured myself into the task of building a full, multimedia *Ponce* presentation, complete with pictures, videos, and music. I'd left the ship with a CD full of magazine-quality photos, which I spread liberally throughout my PowerPoint slides. I selected the choicest episodes from my time aboard, which I wove into the narrative of my improbable journey from new-guy reservist to second-in-command. I painted word portraits of many of the characters I'd encountered and shone a bright spotlight on our harmonica-and-guitar-playing captain.

In the end, I brought it all back to the greatness of the American sailor and the terrific work the men and women of the United States Navy did every day, in far-away places, often in harm's way, without any expectation of thanks or recognition. My goal through it all was to follow the advice I'd been given by the Naval Academy commandant when I'd written speeches for him: Make 'em laugh, make 'em cry, leave 'em feeling good.

No one cried, but it was otherwise a hit. I was the main event at the Wednesday Lunch-And-Learn and delivered my presentation to a packed conference room, a near-record crowd for such an event. I spoke uninterrupted for forty-five minutes and took questions for another fifteen.

The final question came from an older gentleman who usually kept to himself and didn't speak up much in groups. I knew him to be an Air Force veteran and noticed he'd been following my remarks closely.

He politely raised his hand and asked, "How were you able to come back to this?"

"This?" I asked.

"Yes, this. How were you able to return to this setting after the experience you described?"

Ah, *this*. It clicked. Put another way, the question was, "How did you have the stomach to return to this low-stakes bullshit after serving in a key leadership role in an organization doing high-stakes, frequently dangerous work in a region of vital importance to US national interest?"

It was an insightful, penetrating question . . . that I promptly dodged.

"Well, you know, I took some time off to catch up with the family and lounge around the pool. It didn't take me too long to get back into my usual routine."

The gentleman deserved a better answer, but there was no way I was going down that path in that setting. No way was I baring my soul to that crowd. Had the two of us been enjoying a few beers at the local VFW, I would have told him, "Actually, it's pretty frickin' miserable coming back to this place to be reminded every day how ridiculous my existence is here and in the civilian world in general. Coming back makes me feel small and insignificant, that I'm letting myself down. I feel like I'm wasting my talents and squandering what should be the most productive years of my life. Does that answer your question?"

I tried to give him a look that said, "I get it. You're exactly right. But that's a discussion for another day." Thankfully, he let the matter drop.

Part of me hoped—fantasized—that members of the company leadership team in the audience would get together later and say, "Geez, our eyes have been opened! We're totally under-utilizing Dan. It's a waste of his time and ours for him to do marketing communications. What else should he be doing?" And then I'd promptly be moved into a role of actual consequence to the business.

But it was not to be. Instead, the message from my boss was, "Nice presentation. Now go get your fucking shine box!"

As soon as I'd returned, I knew my days in the organization were numbered. I saw no opportunity to improve my situation, although

I wasn't looking too hard for one. Even among those who thought they knew what I was *supposed* to be doing as a strategic marketing consultant, I'd been typecast as a communications guy. That was damning, and I knew it.

I began the job search in earnest, starting with conversations with a few friends to determine exactly what I wanted in a new role. First, I had to shake the communications stink from my resume. Second, I wanted to put my high-priced MBA to use. Next, I wanted to lead people. It occurred to me that I'd only been an individual contributor as a civilian, even though every bit of my military education, training, and experience had prepared me to be the dude in charge of something . . . anything. I didn't expect to step right into a CEO role, but it wasn't unreasonable to imagine there was some company out there that might be interested to have me run even a small corner of its operation.

"Absolutely," according to a buddy's father-in-law I'd contacted through my networking effort. "You should check out the railroad."

The railroad? I'd never considered it, but it quickly made sense. My friend's father-in-law had been an Air Force F-4 Phantom pilot in Vietnam and had a career in the railroad after leaving the military. He pointed out that I already had wide experience leading groups of blue-collar guys who turned wrenches on large, dangerous pieces of equipment. That's what I had done in my squadron days and continued to do aboard *Ponce*. They were roles I'd enjoyed and, apparently, had direct parallels to the railroad.

"I think you'd find railroaders to be a lot like sailors," he continued. The more we talked, the more the whole idea appealed to me. The way I saw it, the railroad stood at the opposite end of the spectrum from corporate public affairs and marketing communications. That alone gave the idea significant merit. And if railroaders did indeed resemble sailors, then I should be right at home. Yes, this was a terrific idea.

As it turned out, one of his former proteges was the chief operating officer at one of the class one railroads, among the largest in the country as measured by annual revenues. He was a West Point graduate, former Army helicopter pilot, and always on the lookout for new talent. Would I be interested in an introduction?

Umm, is the Pope Catholic?

Emails were exchanged, a call was scheduled, and an invitation for an interview was extended. A week later, I traveled to the railroad's headquarters to meet Mike, the COO, in person, as well as several members of his team. The conversations were extremely enjoyable because they focused primarily on leadership. And there were several veterans in the organization, many of whom I met during a tour of the railroad's operations center. I surmised the visit was going well when I later found myself in the CEO's office for a personal conversation. He was extremely cordial and spoke to me as though I already worked there. *That's a hell of a good sign*, I thought.

The day after I returned home, I received a call from the vice president of HR. He made me a verbal offer for the role of assistant vice president, mechanical operations. I was to have responsibility for all railcar maintenance operations, including several facilities and a couple of hundred employees, or car men, in railroad parlance. I almost couldn't believe it. Was I really being forgiven for the sins of my communications past? Was I really being offered an opportunity for a fresh start?

I accepted almost immediately. A short time later, I called one of my Naval Academy classmates to share the news. Unlike me, he had made all the right moves to land in all the right places after leaving active duty, including the University of Chicago Graduate School of Business, a junior partnership at McKinsey, and a corporate vice presidency. When I told him about my new role, he said, "Oh . . . You finally got yourself a big-boy job. Good for you!"

That's right! A big-boy job. The next person I wanted to tell was my boss. *See!* I wanted to say. *Someone out there takes me seriously. Look at that title . . . Assistant Vice President! Shit-hot, right?* But the actual conversation that took place when I resigned was pretty tame, even friendly. Truth be told, the boss was a damn nice guy. Aside from the communication plan-writing, I had to admit he'd been good to me. I had no designs on a take-this-job-and-shove-it kind of departure. We chatted for a bit about my new role, and then he shook my hand and wished me luck.

And, like all the civilian bosses I'd had before him, he was visibly relieved to be getting rid of me.

It was unusual for the railroad to bring in an outsider to fill a senior role. The COO was taking a risk on me, and I fully appreciated and respected that. And in what I thought was not only a classy, but also a highly pragmatic move, Mike shipped me off to three months of training before I even stepped foot on the railroad's property. One of the other class one railroads had a training center set up at the local community college, where I was enrolled in several introductory-level courses. Mike didn't expect ninety days of course work to fully bridge the knowledge gap that would exist between me and the experienced railroaders I would lead. He just wanted me to speak the language. That struck me as highly reasonable, and I was again grateful for his very enlightened approach to my onboarding.

I was a highly motivated student. I showed up the first day of class about thirty minutes early, fully charged coffee mug in hand, wearing my freshly pressed khakis, button-down oxford shirt, and LL Bean moccasins. *Be casual*, I thought. I wanted to look like a serious student, but not one who was trying too hard. *Blend in. Just play it cool.*

After a while, my classmates began to trickle in. Each wore the same uniform: jeans, boots, tee shirt, and a tattered ball cap. And each looked at me as though I had just landed from one of the moons of Jupiter. By the time the class started, there wasn't another pair of khakis or moccasins to be found anywhere in the entire building. The guys looked sideways at me as though I were a DEA informant sent to spy on them. "Who the fuck is *this* guy?" said the look on each of their faces. So much for blending in.

The next day, I had myself squared away in the proper uniform. As time went on, the suspicion from the other students waned and they started to accept me. Clearly, I was not destined to be a car man, like they were. When asked about my job, I was vague. "You know, something in management," I'd say. I explained I was former military, as a few of them were, had been working in the corporate world for a while, and had been offered a job with the railroad. Since I was an outsider, my boss wanted to get me up to speed as quickly as possible, so he thought I should start in the classroom. They all agreed this made good sense, and we got along just fine.

As a parting act of goodwill, I wore my khakis on the last day of class, just to let them give me shit. And they did. My buddy's father-in-law was right, I thought. These railroaders were my kind of folks.

A few weeks later, I was sitting in the Saturday morning operations conference call at the company headquarters. I wasn't big on work-life balance, so I was happy to be back in an organization that worked weekends. Around the table were various members of the mechanical and transportation departments, as well as a handful of others from elsewhere in the company. The call took place every day, except Sunday, at 7:00 a.m. and covered every aspect of railroad operations—equipment status, track conditions, the status of high-priority cargo, the weather, etc. It resembled the daily operations-intelligence briefing held aboard warships.

Mike, the COO, wandered down from his office to sit in. He nodded along, asked a few questions, and shuffled a small pile of papers in front of him. At the end of the call, after those who'd dialed in had checked off, he made what I thought a peculiar comment to those of us in the room.

"By the way, despite any rumors you may have heard to the contrary, I'm not getting fired."

There was some awkward laughter, a couple of "ah, bullshits!" and then the meeting broke up.

I had no idea what Mike was talking about. And as the newest guy there, I wasn't about to go asking around, either. *Such a strange comment*, I thought.

The following Wednesday, I was back in the conference room for the daily operations update. This time, near the end of the discussion, the CEO wandered in. I'd heard he sat in occasionally, but, judging from the others' surprised reactions, he didn't do so very often. When the call ended, the CEO spoke up.

"You, you, and you . . . *stay.*"

He'd pointed to the vice presidents seated around the table. The rest of us were clearly expected to leave, immediately. We all got the message and high-tailed it out of the conference room. A few minutes later, Gerard stuck his head in my cubicle. "Could you come down to my office for a minute?"

Gerard was my boss, the vice president of mechanical operations. Mike had hired him shortly after he'd hired me. I'd had very little interaction with him to that point. He was about fifteen years older than I and had spent most of his thirty-year career in the railroad. I walked down to his office, where I found my peers, the two other assistance vice presidents in the mechanical department.

Gerard looked a little shell-shocked as he closed the door behind me. He gave it an extra nudge to make sure it was completely closed.

"So . . . umm . . . Mike was let go."

What?

The chief operating officer had been fired. That was the message the CEO had delivered in the conference room. He hadn't offered why, of course, but did say he expected Mike to get fully *lawyered up.* In the meantime, everyone should just carry on as usual.

I was dumbfounded. Carry on as usual? I was brand new. I had no idea what *usual* was. Mike had told me he didn't expect me to fully take the reins in my new role without first traveling the network to get to know the workers. "Take your time," he'd said, without specifying exactly how long. That very week, I'd intended to present Mike a formal transition plan to try to nail down the details, but never got the opportunity. I suppose I could present the plan to Gerard, but he was in the same boat as I. Neither of us had gotten a lot of guidance from Mike. When I mentioned my plan to Gerard, he didn't seem the least bit interested. "Sure . . . whatever," was his reaction. He had his own issues to work out.

So, I hit the road. *Create some positive momentum*, I told myself. *Go meet some people. Go learn some stuff.* Mike had made no formal announcement that I had joined the company, so most people I encountered had no idea who I was.

"Nice to meet you. I'm Dan, the new guy in the mechanical department. I look forward to working with you." That's how I started most conversations.

"Okay . . . and what exactly do you do?" Still unsure whether I could give a straight answer, I usually replied with, "You know, I'll be working with Chet and Randy back at headquarters, doing something on the leadership team. We're still sorting out the details." I'm sure it sounded like complete bullshit.

The truth was, I had no idea whether I would ever assume the role for which I was hired. Urban legend held that when an executive was fired, there typically followed a purge of those most closely aligned with him. Mike and I weren't close, but he was the entire reason I was hired. And I'm sure, given my non-railroad background, that had raised more than a few eyebrows. Without his executive sponsorship, I assumed I was vulnerable.

I wasn't about to share that with my wife. We'd packed up and sold our house, bought a new one, and had just finished unpacking the last box. Neither she nor my daughter had wanted to move.

"Who cares if you don't like your job?" she'd asked. "Nobody likes his job. We're happy here. Get over it."

Even after I explained all the wonderful things I thought the new job would do for my career and how much healthier my outlook would be after a fresh start, she'd wanted nothing to do with it.

So I kept my mouth shut and tried to keep busy. I traveled. I studied. I sat in on meetings. Gerard continued to show zero interest in me, so I continued in this purgatory for almost two months. Then I was invited—directed—to join a discussion for which I had little interest or understanding.

Enterprise Resource Planning, or ERP, is the software that drives a business. And an ERP implementation is a business activity that often wrecks careers. I'd read a case study in my operations management class at Harvard that detailed the many ways ERP implementations become complete train wrecks for organizations. They're always over budget. They never follow anyone's notion of a reasonable timeline. And someone in the organization is always scapegoated and made to pay.

"This is Dan. He's going to be our business sponsor."

Dave, the chief information officer, made the announcement to the IT consultants, vendor reps, and members of the IT team assembled.

"He'll report directly to the steering committee and will be responsible to get this done on time and on budget."

It was the first I'd heard of any of this. ERP implementation? How in the hell was I qualified to do that?

Then it occurred to me. This is how I'd be run out of the organization. I imagined the discussion among the members of the executive office.

"What the hell? This thing's already a disaster. Let the new kid try. We have nothing to lose."

I certainly didn't feel poised for success. But I wasn't being asked to write communications plans, either.

No more shines, Billy.

LESSONS LEARNED

1.   1. I *liked* myself in the role of executive officer, more so than in any previous role I'd held. That was gift. And it came about almost entirely by luck. I could not have foreseen the unique

set of circumstances or supporting cast of characters that came together at that moment in time to provide me the tailor-made, best-fit opportunity I so thoroughly enjoyed.

In my time since *Ponce*, I've made numerous attempts to deconstruct the experience, understand its core elements, and then either find or recreate them in a private-sector role. And I have failed, repeatedly. Some opportunities are too unique to be replicated. This was one.

2. Beware of made-up-sounding titles. My boss may have had a clear idea of the roles and responsibilities of the strategic marketing consultant. But I sure as hell didn't. And neither did anyone else in the organization. I bore some responsibility to define the role, and I made a few half-hearted attempts to do so. But, given my public affairs background, I was quickly typecast as a communications guy. Any attempt I made to work my way farther up the corporate value chain was met with "Go get your shine box." One would hope titles wouldn't matter so much. But my experience suggests they absolutely do.

3. Don't expect the person who hired you to carry you to success. He or she might not even be around tomorrow. An opportunity should stand on its own merits, irrespective of who provided it. Be sure it's structurally sound enough in terms of industry or functional fit to move you forward in your career, no matter who is or isn't standing in your corner. Ask yourself whether the odds are favorable enough this role will enable you to grow and develop in meaningful ways, no matter whom you work for. Executive sponsorship is nice to have but should not be the sole basis for accepting a new position.

Gerard

**"Your communication has been lacking.
That needs to improve—immediately!"**

On the railroad, 2014.

My survival required that I be an IT guy. That was an unexpected twist. But I'd faked my way through plenty of other roles. And who knew? Maybe I'd last long enough to pick up a quality resume bullet. It never hurt to have another war story for those "Tell me about a time when . . ." interview questions.

And I fully expected to be interviewing again, soon. Success wasn't an impossibility, but it was unlikely. I was an outsider. The guy who'd stuck his neck out to hire me was gone. I'd just been served one of the largest shit sandwiches of my career. And my boss could not be bothered with me.

I was told I would be fully dedicated to the ERP implementation. Still, I reported to Gerard. At first, I considered that a positive. Maybe this IT thing was temporary, and I would soon move on to the job I was hired to do in the mechanical department. Maybe I was the sacrificial offering Gerard was forced to make when the CEO went around the table to all the VPs and said, "All right. One of you guys is going to cough up a body to run this goddamn ERP implementation.

Who's it going to be?" Maybe he desperately wanted me to assume my duties as assistant vice president but had been overruled. That had to be the case, right?

No, it did not. Two days after I was stuck with the ERP implementation, Gerard announced Randy, one of the other AVPs, was taking over railcar operations. I was out. And things got weird, fast.

Nearly all the target users of the new IT system were members of the mechanical department. Almost nothing was automated in the shops, and some form of digital maintenance management was long overdue. Of course, this was intended to make life easier for the people doing the work, but Gerard wasn't so convinced. Even despite being a member of the steering committee, he made it immediately clear that he was against the project. He thought things were fine the way they were. He didn't like the vendor and thought we'd been scammed. He didn't like the consultants the CIO had hired to manage portions of the implementation. He didn't like the people on the project team and thought they had no idea what went on inside the mechanical department. And, in time, he didn't like me. I was to become the embodiment of every evil this project conjured for Gerard.

I got my first hint during a steering committee meeting. The CIO was adamant we had to focus on end-user buy-in.

"The folks in the shop have to *want* to use this. We'll fail if we don't win hearts and minds. What are you guys doing about that?"

I completely agreed and detailed the team's plan to co-opt shop leaders in the design process. The CIO seemed satisfied, as did the other members of the committee—except for Gerard.

"I had dinner with Ben earlier this week." Ben managed the largest locomotive shop in our network.

"He said there's no way a bunch of guys who don't even use smart phones are going to use this system. They're all thinking, 'Hey, there's nothing broken here. What are we trying to fix? This is just something the corporate suits are doing to make themselves look good.' I told Ben, 'I don't disagree one bit.'"

Gerard then dismissively threw his hands out in front of his chest and concluded with, "So there you have it."

Wait a minute. Ben, one of the guys whose buy-in was most critical to the project's success, was concerned with end-user adoption. And rather than allay his concerns, Gerard instead actively encouraged them. Was I the only one hearing this?

Apparently so. The CIO turned to me and said, "Okay, Dan. So I guess you have a problem. Winning hearts and minds is going to be harder than you thought. You'd better rethink your approach." None of the other committee members seemed to disagree.

Rethink my approach? How about instead Gerard keep his goddamned mouth shut and not chop my legs out from under me?

I was pissed. The tops of my ears started to burn. I took a breath, and as calmly and diplomatically as I could, replied, "Yes, I understand this will be a challenge. But we needn't make it more difficult on ourselves by being openly critical of the project with the crew in the shop. If anyone on this committee has any concerns, I hope those might be kept in this room. When we all leave here, we need to present a united front."

The CIO gave me a look of, "Yeah, whatever," and the meeting broke up soon thereafter.

I thought about catching Gerard on the way out of the conference room. I wanted there to be no disagreement or ambiguity on the need for a united front. Like it or not, the organization had chosen to move forward with the project, and so should he. But I was still pissed and assumed my diplomatic tank had run dry. In such a state, things could turn confrontational, exactly what I didn't need. So I let it go.

A week later, I forwarded an invitation to Gerard for one of the design sessions the consultants had arranged with some of the workers from the shop. I thought it would give him a great opportunity to get some first-hand feedback on what the early obstacles to adoption among members of our end-user population might be. He was traveling quite a bit, and I really didn't expect him to attend, but I least wanted him to know it was happening. I walked down the hall after hitting *send* on the invite and stuck my head in his office.

"I just forwarded you an invite. Not sure what your schedule looks like, but I wanted to keep you in the loop. We're getting some of the folks from the car shop together to give us some input on the design for their module. Should be a good discussion."

"Thanks. Honestly, I'm not even sure where I'm going to be that week. But I'll keep it in mind." Fair enough. Gerard was a busy guy.

As expected, he did not attend. The Monday morning following the event, I was sitting at my desk when an email from Gerard popped into my in-box. I could see from the subject line it had to do with the design session. The consultants had sent around a summary to all steering committee members. The event had gone quite well, I thought, yielding some terrific feedback that led to changes we were able to incorporate into the system design almost immediately. Gerard was probably passing along an atta-boy, I assumed.

Nope.

"It would have been nice to know about this *in advance*. This is something I should have attended. Your communication has been lacking. That needs to improve—immediately!"

I caught a chill as the color ran out of my face. Was Gerard serious? Not only had I forwarded him the invitation, but I'd also told him about it. In person. To his face. Standing in his office. This had to be a misunderstanding. There was no other plausible explanation.

I grabbed a copy of Gerard's email off of the printer and headed straight to his office.

He's a busy guy, I told myself. *He gets pulled in a lot of different directions. He can't possibly remember every detail of every day. He probably just forgot. He's human.*

"Gerard, do you have a minute?"

"Yes." His curt reply had the same ominous tone as his email.

I held out the copy of his message. "I'm a little confused. I sent you the invite for this and then told you about it right here in your office. I know you're busy, but I'm not sure what else I could have done to communicate this to you."

Gerard took off his reading glasses and glared directly at me.

"I don't appreciate being lectured by you in front of the entire steering committee about your 'united front.' If you have some kind of problem, you either need to address it with me in private or keep your mouth shut. I will not have you embarrass me like that again."

United front? Now I was really confused. I thought the issue was the design session he'd missed. Was he talking about the steering committee meeting from two weeks ago? If so, why now? Why hadn't he said anything sooner?

"Uh . . . okay." It took me a minute to gather my thoughts. "Well, that's a fair point. And I certainly didn't mean to embarrass you. I was just concerned that our job's going to be a lot more difficult if you aren't supporting us within the shop."

"Yeah, well, it's not my job to convince anyone of anything about this project. That's yours. So just do your job and keep your editorial comments to yourself."

Gerard put on his glasses and turned toward his computer. Ass-chewing complete. Dismissed.

I walked out of his office, still confused. It was easily the most bizarre exchange I'd ever had with a boss.

Clearly, I would need to manage Gerard very carefully. I was still the new kid, and he was my boss. He had the upper hand. But if he was going to level accusations against me about things I had or hadn't said, or the manner in which I had or hadn't said them, then I would need to protect myself. I started saving copies of every email I sent him, and those he sent me, both electronic and hard copy.

It's always a sad moment when one starts saving a boss's emails. As I'd learned in the past, it typically marked the beginning of the end of the relationship.

Gerard wasn't my only problem. There was also Peter, the project manager our software vendor had assigned us. For the life of me, I couldn't get a straight answer out of the guy.

"Hey, Peter, you owed us an updated version of the inbound railcar inspection module yesterday. Why didn't we get it?"

"Well, you know . . . when I put that date on the project plan, I wasn't entirely sure which of our coders would be available to work on it."

"Hey, Peter, our next conference room pilot kicks off Monday, and I haven't seen any of the prototypes or prep materials. Where do we stand on those?"

"Well, you know . . . I'm sure we'll have everything ready by then."

It was infuriating. I didn't know anything about IT, but I knew how to keep deadlines. Peter didn't, *despite being a project manager*. When I got fed up enough, I elevated the issue of missed deadlines to our vendor's vice president who had responsibility for our project. She didn't seem the least bit concerned.

"Peter's one of our best," she'd say. "We've given you one of our best."

Even our own CIO seemed unconcerned. "Those are just milestones," he'd say. "It's okay if they slide a bit."

Are you kidding me? If this was typical of how organizations managed ERP implementations, it was no wonder they were always overdue and over-budget.

I couldn't accept it. Such sloppiness was anathema to me. I concluded a conference call during which I'd stated my dissatisfaction with Peter's performance in no uncertain terms with, "Fix it, or we'll be finding a new project manager."

"Well, I think he finally got the message," said David, a member of the project team. I appreciated the encouraging words. I was beginning to feel as though I were the only one who gave a shit about meeting deadlines.

Then I noticed Kathleen, one of the sharpest engineers on the project, smiling at me from across the conference room table. For whatever reason, she loved to harass me. We got along quite well.

"Ooooh . . . I love it when Dan uses his *Navy* voice."

The entire room erupted. We'd become a pretty tight team, and any comment that made light of an otherwise trying situation was always welcome. Everyone thought Kathleen's comment was hilarious.

I laughed along, too, but without completely getting the joke. What exactly did she mean by my *Navy voice?* I'd left active duty almost a decade before.

After the meeting ended, I decided to ask.

"*Navy* voice . . . what the hell does that mean?"

"You know . . . that voice you use when you're mad. Very stern, very direct . . . all deep and everything. Isn't that how all military people talk to each other?"

Now *that* was funny. Like countless civilians before her, Kathleen assumed life in the military resembled what was depicted in *Full Metal Jacket*. No one had normal conversations. Everyone shouted "Sir, yes, sir!" and ran around in formation wearing combat boots.

"Is that what you really think?" She couldn't be serious.

"Well . . . I don't know. Maybe." Kathleen was a highly intelligent person, and she was likely just pulling my chain. But I could tell part of her did, in fact, believe life in the military was like *Full Metal Jacket*.

Kathleen didn't understand me. Peter couldn't meet deadlines. And things continued to deteriorate with Gerard.

A pattern emerged: I would brief Gerard on an issue, both in person and via email, and he would then promptly forget. Later that night, usually around ten o'clock, after he'd knocked back a few bourbons, he would send me an excoriating email to take me to task for failing to keep him informed, carbon copying every member of my team. I would read the email early the following morning, panic, race to the office, gather copies of all the emails I had sent pertaining to the topic, and take them to Gerard's office. Once there, I would present him all the evidence that I had indeed informed him of whatever the issue, remind him of our conversation on the same topic, and then inquire as to what may have been the disconnect. His typical reply would be, "Oh. Okay. Thanks." Eventually, I started to take people with me to these discussions, just to have a witness. Either Gerard was suffering from dementia or was an alcoholic. Maybe both.

Whatever the case, it was not a healthy situation. The project team and I were making steady progress on the ERP implementation, but gaining end-user buy-in remained a persistent challenge, particularly as Gerard continued to undermine our efforts to do so at every turn. The other members of the steering committee remained unaware of this, or simply didn't care. When I tried to gently broach the topic with the vice president of application development, a person I'd come to respect and admire, he brushed it off with, "Well, Dan, you're definitely in a tricky spot, but that's just the way these things go." He had his own problems and didn't want to add Gerard to his list.

So, I drank. A lot. And I didn't sleep much. I kept my regular workout schedule, but all the stress, booze, and railroader's diet of fried-everything started taking a toll.

"What the hell?" I'd mutter to myself as I tried to button my pants. "These damn things must have shrunk at the dry cleaners."

I started to dread every morning, because I knew as soon as I picked up my phone, I'd discover a fresh zinger from Gerard. His Jekyll-and-Hyde persona was wearing me down. I tried to console myself with the simple absurdity of the situation. *This is crazy. It can't go on like this.* But then I'd remind myself that he was my boss, had me by the balls, and no one else in the company seemed to notice or care. It could indeed go on. There was no relief in sight.

About a year into the experience, a friend of a friend passed me contact information for Jeff, a fellow Naval Academy graduate. He was a group president for an industrial manufacturer in town and managed a pretty sizeable portfolio.

"You guys would hit it off," my acquaintance had said. "Give him a call."

But I was in no hurry to do so. I was busy managing my Gerard situation, and I already knew plenty of Annapolis grads. One more wasn't going to make any difference. So I filed Jeff's info away and forgot about it.

Six months later, I was invited to interview with a holding company that hired veterans almost exclusively to manage its businesses. I assumed I wanted to run a business and thought I understood all that it entailed. But truth be told, I really didn't. Time spent in corporate public affairs, marketing, and railroad IT really hadn't given me any useful insights on business leadership. I'd read about it but had neither experienced it nor observed it up close. Maybe this fellow Academy grad could share some insights that would both validate my interest in running a business and confirm my suitability to do so. I dug out his contact info, shot off an introductory email, and asked for a meeting.

Jeff obliged, and I found the acquaintance who connected us to have been exactly right. We hit it off immediately. Here was a guy who'd known nothing but success since leaving the active duty Navy but didn't judge me for the total absence of it in my own civilian career.

"Taking you a while to figure it out, huh? Yeah, that happens. You'll get there."

I told him about the opportunity for which I was interviewing and asked about his own experience running businesses.

"Nothing else I'd rather do," he said. And he confirmed my Navy experience had already provided me the fundamentals to be successful doing the same.

"You'd do great. Go for it."

I left Jeff's office with renewed confidence. But, unfortunately, that confidence wasn't enough to yield a successful outcome at the interview the following week. I learned most veterans the company hired started out as project managers in one of the portfolio businesses at a meager salary. And only after two or three years of success in such a role were they then considered for a leadership opportunity.

"So what if it takes you a few years to get an opportunity to run a business?" the CEO asked. "Does that change how you think about us?"

I had to be honest. "Yes," I replied. "I'd say this probably isn't a good fit."

The CEO agreed. When the recruiter called the day after I returned from the interview, he shared the feedback and thanked me for my honesty. "But let's keep in touch," he said. They always say that.

As a courtesy, I emailed Jeff with a debrief of the experience and thanked him again for our conversation.

"Sorry it didn't work out," he replied. Then he followed with something that caught me completely off guard. "If you're open to a change, what do you think about checking us out? We should talk again."

I was blown away. I hadn't contacted Jeff in search of an opportunity, just some friendly advice. But there it was. For the first time, I imagined life without Gerard. And that life looked pretty damn good.

I readily agreed to another meeting. Jeff suggested that before we talk again, I meet his HR director. She could explain the role he had in mind for me, and then he would follow up to answer any questions.

"That okay with you?" he asked.

Hell, yes. One does not meet the HR director unless the opportunity is real.

Jeff had an opening for a vice president of sales. He knew I had no sales experience but suggested that this would be a good developmental role. That made terrific sense. My Dad spent his career in sales and had always told me no one who runs a business should be without such experience.

"You need to do time out on the front lines and get punched in the face by some customers. There's no substitute for it." Sound advice.

Things moved quickly. I did a round of interviews in Jeff's local office and then flew to his corporate headquarters for interviews there.

Given my early experience at the railroad, I kept asking myself, *If Jeff were to disappear tomorrow, would I still consider this a good opportunity? Would I still have a reasonable chance at success?*

The company served a thriving, global industry; leaders of portfolio businesses were given wide autonomy to run them as they saw fit; and success in the sales role could lead to an opportunity to lead one of those businesses. There would always be the risk things weren't what they appeared. You couldn't truly judge an organization until you were in it. And you couldn't get around the fact that sometimes weird shit happened to people and businesses beyond anyone's control. But I ultimately concluded that, whatever the risk, I shouldn't pass this up.

I called Jeff from the airport after my meeting with the CEO.

"It went well from my perspective. If you and your team are interested in moving forward, then so am I."

Back at the railroad, I was two months into my quasi-new role in the mechanical department. In addition to leading the ERP implementation, it was decided Randy and I would share responsibility for railcar operations. The network was split in half geographically. Randy took the southern half, and I took the northern. I had no idea whose idea this arrangement was, but I doubted it was Gerard's. I couldn't imagine him making any such accommodation for me. While I was somewhat gratified to finally get at least a portion of the job for which I was hired, the role required expanded interaction with Gerard and made me further subject to his mania.

On the bright side, I thoroughly enjoyed my interaction with the guys in the shops. As my buddy's father-in-law had suggested, railroaders were indeed a lot like sailors. They were honest, genuine, hard-working, and generous. Many had fathers, grandfathers, and great-grandfathers who had also worked in the railroad and were extremely proud of this heritage. It was energizing to be around them.

But the benefits of the new role failed to outweigh the costs of continuing with Gerard. When I informed him that I was leaving, he responded with, "Was it something I said?"

Are you shitting me? I thought. *Where do I even begin?*

I was due to start my new role with Jeff on a Monday. Rather than choosing the preceding Friday as my last day at the railroad, I chose Sunday. There wasn't anything planned beyond ordinary operations that weekend, so why not collect another two days' pay?

Sure enough, my phone rang at three o'clock on Sunday morning. A couple of railcars had derailed at one of our yards. There were no injuries or significant damage, but the cars had derailed in such a manner as to require contractors to come in with special equipment to get the cars back on the track. Such work would be expensive on a Sunday morning, but it had to be done. The derailment was snarling a portion of the traffic through the yard. After he'd briefed me on the situation, I told the manager who'd called me to start making the necessary arrangements with the contractors and asked that he update me in a few hours.

Such incidents were fairly common. Rather than call Gerard, I sent him a brief text message—usually his preferred method of communication. I concluded it by saying I would call him later that morning with a comprehensive brief once I'd been updated by the manager on the scene. Then I put down my phone and went back to sleep.

I spoke with the manager again around eight o'clock that morning and called Gerard immediately afterwards.

"Sounds like you're doing all the right things," he said. "Thanks." He didn't seem the least bit concerned.

It took a while to get the contractors on site, which wasn't unusual for a Sunday. Finally, around six o'clock that evening, the cars were back on the rail and traffic resumed its normal flow through the yard. I shot Gerard a text message to let him know all was back to normal.

A few hours later, I received a summary of the entire incident via email from the manager, which I then forwarded to Gerard.

Early the next morning, I was sitting in my home office drinking coffee, thinking through the day ahead, my first in my new job. Just for the hell of it, despite no longer being a railroad employee, I checked my email to see if anything interesting had happened overnight. Old habits.

There was an email from Gerard. In reply to the incident summary I'd forwarded the night before, Gerard wrote, "What's happening with this, Dan? Need some leadership here! I need you to communicate with me!" And, of course, he'd copied every member of my team.

Unbelievable. Another one for the Gerard file.

LESSONS LEARNED

1. It's always a bad idea to attempt to correct your boss in public. Always. Especially in front of his peers. Even if you're right. Unless he's about to drop bombs on the wrong target, whatever correction you think your boss requires can wait. Only do it after careful consideration and *always* in private. I'd learned this lesson a long time before, but had apparently forgotten.

2. When you start saving your boss's emails to cover your ass, it's the beginning of the end. One of you is leaving. And it will probably be you. So be sure your resume is updated, your contacts are current, and your house is otherwise in order when it reaches that point.

3. It's an employee's responsibility to *manage up* and build a productive relationship with his boss. But there are limits. If the boss's behavior veers off into the inappropriate or irrational, seek the advice of an HR professional. You may be in a situation you can't fix.

King John

"Don't make an executive at my level have to guess what he's reading."

Corporate America, 2018.

"You guys should come up and have a look."

King John really wanted us to see his throne room, the newly refurbished cabin of his Gulfstream G550. He was a senior executive with the company that had recently acquired the one for which I had worked, and, according to the new org chart, was my boss's boss.

I couldn't have given a shit less about his Gulfstream. All I wanted was for King John to leave. And I was pretty sure Chet, my sales director, felt the same.

"Well, John, we know you're busy. And it looks like we've gotten you behind schedule. We can see it another time." *Shit, I hope not.*

"Naw, we're fine. These guys won't leave without me." John motioned in the direction of the pilots in the cockpit. He stood at the top of the ladder at the entrance to the cabin. Chet and I stood below on the tarmac.

It was clear we weren't getting out of a tour. "Okay. Sure."

Chet and I started up the stairs while John moved inside. By the time we joined him, he'd already gotten situated in the prime seat in the cabin. I'd flown on a corporate jet once before, and I knew where one sat was indicative of one's rank. Important guys sat facing forward near the front of the aircraft. Less important guys sat facing backwards, usually in back. John's seat was about a third of the way back from the forward-most bulkhead, facing forward, on the right side. He was clearly the *big shit* on that plane.

Chet and I looked around, feigning interest. "Not bad, John. This looks very . . . comfortable."

I almost hoped John would jump out of his seat and give us the grand tour, like a kid showing off his new fort.

"Check this out . . . look at the wood paneling in that lavatory! And look how far back these seats recline. You can sleep all the way to Beijing on this thing. And how did they get a cupholder there? Friggin' awesome, right?"

Instead, John looked casually over his shoulder and replied, "Yeah, it's okay."

Get excited over something as pedestrian as a corporate jet? Come on . . . only guys as low-ranking and insignificant as Chet and me would do that.

I'd witnessed such a display before. One of the lasting lessons from my Naval Academy experience was that one should proactively engage the professor of a course with which one was struggling *before* one's grade started to suffer. I'd thus made an appointment with my business strategy professor at Harvard, hoping to get some insight as to why his class made such little sense to me. I just wasn't getting it.

I found him to be a bloviating, pompous asshole in the classroom, but assumed he would be more agreeable in a one-on-one setting. Wrong. Soon after I arrived for my appointment and explained my difficulties, he pulled one of Michael Porter's books off his shelf. Porter, the world-renowned author of the *Five Forces of Competitive Position Analysis*, was a Harvard Business School legend. Thinking perhaps there was some nugget of Porter wisdom that my professor wanted to impart, I was disappointed, but not surprised, when he instead said, "Porter actually mentions my name in this book. Let's see, where is that . . ." And then I sat for several minutes until he found the passage. It was awkward. And embarrassing.

So was this.

Chet and I stood there for a few uncomfortable seconds before I offered, "Well, John, we appreciated the visit. We'll pull together the answers to your questions and get them to you by the end of the week."

"You guys have some work to do. I hope we have a very different conversation the next time I'm here." John was once again the lecturing, condescending prick he'd been in the conference room an hour prior.

"Okay. Safe travels."

Next time? I doubted I'd be around to see any *next time.* I assumed my days were numbered. This corporation had wrecked my business, and John had made it abundantly clear he considered it all my fault. In an act of near-fratricide, our new owners had clumsily shuttered one of my manufacturing facilities, creating extended interruptions in the supply chains of my customers that had thrown them into open revolt. I'd had nothing to do with the decision, but had been left to clean up the mess.

I hadn't seen any of this coming twenty-four months prior. Things had started out great in my new vice president of sales role. I'd had a lot to learn but was eager and grateful for the opportunity to do so. I'd inherited a dedicated team of industry veterans that, rather than look askance at me, readily accepted me and went to great lengths to ensure I avoided any serious missteps early on. My immediate boss, Byron, our business unit's general manager, proved just as supportive as the rest of the team. And Jeff checked in regularly to ensure I was getting up to speed without too much difficulty.

Finally! I thought. *A* normal *work situation.*

Until it wasn't. Three months after I started, Byron was abruptly reassigned, requiring Jeff to step in as interim general manager. Three months after that, it was announced that the holding company to which we all reported was to be acquired by a Fortune 500 behemoth.

"It's about to get a lot more corporate around here," Jeff had said.

Two months following the announcement, two of my most senior salespeople got raging drunk at a conference in Las Vegas and sexually harassed and threatened a group of coworkers. I suspended them the next day. Two months after that, Jeff promoted me to take full responsibility for one of his portfolio businesses. *Yes!* A month later, he announced two other businesses would be combined with mine to form a new business unit that I would lead. *Yes!* A month later, it was announced that the manufacturing facility for one of those businesses would be shut down, all assets would be moved to my main facility, and all employees in the legacy facility would be laid off. *No!* So went my first year.

It was chaos. And I loved it. I'd long harbored a nagging sense I had squandered an entire decade following business school and that I needed to make up for lost time. Jeff had thrown me right in the frying pan, allowing me an opportunity to do just that. There was no script to suggest any proper course of action to address the various challenges my team and I confronted. But as long as we ensured our actions aligned to a set of clear priorities, made well informed and timely decisions, thoughtfully managed resources, and kept Jeff up to speed on the most important issues, we managed just fine. On any given day, I was fully engaged on a wide set of problems, had reason to draw from numerous parts of my education and experience, and gained incrementally more credibility with my team. It was precisely the sort of leadership challenge I had wanted since leaving the active duty Navy.

We didn't hear much from our new corporate parent until it came time to shut down the plant and relocate the equipment. I was completely naïve as to the difficulty of a such an undertaking, but didn't think much of it.

"We've done this a hundred times," said the leaders of the corporate transition team. "Just follow the playbook, and you'll be fine."

According to the playbook, the whole thing would take ninety days. The receiving facility would undergo the necessary structural modifications, the equipment would be moved and put back in operation, and a new production team would be hired and fully trained, all in three months. The days would be long, and weekends either short or nonexistent, but the plan was absolutely achievable.

"We speak from experience," the corporate guys assured us. "Like we said, we've done this a hundred times."

No one from my team had made any input to the plan, but we took full ownership of it. Several of us made frequent trips to the closing facility to do whatever we could to ease the transition for the employees. No one was happy to be losing their job, but most understood the likelihood the moment the acquisition was announced. There were a handful of key production employees to whom we'd offered an opportunity to relocate, but all had turned us down. Most had extended family in the area. Some simply didn't trust us.

"You're pulling the rug out from underneath us this time. Who's to say you won't do it again?"

It was a fair point. I did some extra explaining and arm-twisting, but to no avail.

Affected employees weren't our only skeptics. I contacted key customers to explain the move plan and the actions we'd be taking to ensure a continuous flow of product during the transition. We would over-produce in the weeks leading up to the move to put enough product on the shelf to cover the ninety-day interruption.

"Ninety days? You sure about that?" was the typical response. "We moved a plant back in '09, and it took a full year before things started getting back to normal."

Yeah, I thought, *but did you have a playbook?*

We started breaking the facility down in early December. Leading the effort was an all-star operations manager the corporation had installed as our project manager. I wasn't thrilled at first to have an outsider in charge, but my attitude quickly changed. I found Mitch's sterling reputation to be well deserved. He was on top of every detail and consistently got stuff done. But he did so without alienating anyone or minimizing any team member's contribution. Mitch approached the move as a collaborative effort that he simply nudged along in a few, targeted areas. While I had expected him to roll in as the all-knowing *corporate guy* and take a very heavy-handed approach to managing the project, I was grateful to experience the exact opposite. Mitch was a gentleman with the highest emotional intelligence. He was a pleasure to work with.

That was fortunate, because the move took a disastrous turn almost the moment the equipment left the building. A huge ice storm blew into the area, halting the semis carrying the equipment for several days. Once they finally made the trip and arrived at the receiving facility, it was discovered several pieces of equipment had broken in transit. So, in addition to setting up and commissioning the equipment in the new location, the project team had to make repairs, blowing the timeline by weeks. And when it came time to fire the machines up, none worked as it was supposed to, requiring several more days of troubleshooting and repairs, conducted by people who had never worked on such equipment. The tribal knowledge that had been lost in our failure to relocate key employees became readily, painfully apparent.

When the equipment finally sputtered to life, we encountered an entirely new set of problems. The raw material ran through the machines well enough, but what emerged as finished product failed to meet our quality specifications by a wide margin. We applied a specialty treatment to a base material that imparted all kinds of novel qualities upon it. Of course, there were numerous variables to be controlled to achieve those qualities, most of which we were either unaware of or didn't know how to adjust. Again, the loss of tribal knowledge was hurting us, badly. We were forced to undergo a months-long process of trial and error by which we slowly learned how to manipulate all the correct inputs to achieve the necessary quality levels for our product. Well—some of the product. In some cases, we simply failed to achieve the same product performance levels in our facility that had been achieved in the previous one. Or it could have been those levels had never been achieved in the first place, and the customers either looked the other way or failed to verify the quality of the goods we provided. We'd discovered evidence to suggest exactly that.

And then there was the fire. Prior to the move, we'd made our own raw material for a portion of our product line, employing a huge, old, medieval-looking furnace in the process. It took several weeks to get it reassembled in the new facility, and we were extremely anxious to get it back online. Some of our most bespoke product required a material produced in-house, and our most important customers were hounding us daily for that product.

"Almost there," we kept telling them. "Any day now."

A group of us happened to be walking through the plant the day the furnace was heating up for a trial run. A second after we passed by it, we heard a loud *pop*. We gave each other the same, quizzical look, and returned to the space that contained the furnace . . . just in time to see flames glowing brightly underneath it. One of our engineers grabbed a fire extinguisher off the wall and quickly went to work extinguishing them. It was a great, heads-up move, I thought, until I saw the large, steel walls of the furnace bulging outwards from the extreme heat and pressure inside. *Shit. This thing might blow.*

"Out!" I shouted. "Everybody out!"

We cleared the entire plant. Soon, smoke was billowing from the roof and the plant's open loading dock doors. For a moment, it looked as though the entire building were going up in flames. The fire department was on the scene in twelve minutes. Firefighters rushed inside, hoses trailing behind them. We all stood a safe distance outside. Everyone had been accounted for, and all we could do was stand there and shiver under an overcast early-March sky.

Eventually, the fire chief emerged from the building and informed us that the fire was out. "Mostly smoke," he said. "Things look okay. We're just monitoring the temperature on the furnace. Still pretty hot in there."

Luckily, our plant manager had hit the emergency kill switch to the furnace on the way out, which likely saved us from a more significant, destructive event.

The postmortem revealed a couple of highly concerning things. First, the person who'd fired up the furnace for the trial hadn't followed proper procedure. He'd failed to ensure proper airflow was present before turning on the burners. Second, there was clear evidence the mechanical safety device that should have caught the error and prevented the burners from being engaged had been deliberately disabled. Whether it was an act of sabotage by a disgruntled employee from the plant we'd closed or simply an ill-thought work-around someone had put in place, we'd never know.

What I did know was that the furnace was damaged beyond repair, would require a half-million bucks to replace, and we wouldn't be making our own material any time soon.

Customers who had been skeptical of our transition plan quickly became furious. We had communicated we'd be back in full production in ninety days, exactly as the playbook had prescribed. But that day had come and gone, and we were unable to say with any certainty when we'd be back to normal production levels.

Every member of the team spent much of their day on conference calls responding to questions like, "What do you mean, you can't say when? What the hell are you guys doing there? You said ninety days. Were you lying to us?"

We'd describe the myriad, unforeseen difficulties we'd encountered and the actions we were taking to address them. My favorite example was the shop floor. Unbeknownst to us, it wasn't level. Some of our machines had large chambers that required tight seals for the treatment process to be effective. With the floors unlevel, the chambers wouldn't seal, and we couldn't make good product. No one had foreseen that.

Soon, customers demanded an audience with King John. Prior to the acquisition, those customers who were squawking the loudest were among our business's smallest and most unprofitable. I wanted to be rid of them. But following the acquisition, those corporate parents of those same customers were among our own new corporation's largest, most profitable customers. They may have represented a miniscule piece of business to us, but they were huge to King John. Terminating them was out of the question. Realizing this, they simply brushed me aside and went straight for the king.

Jeff tried to run interference. When a customer asked for a meeting with John, I deflected him to Jeff. Most of the time, it worked. Jeff was skilled at deescalating such situations, and he successfully placated most customers. And he'd retained an important-enough sounding title that those customers were able to report to their corporate leadership they'd escalated their issues to the highest levels of leadership in our company. Titles mattered in such situations.

Of course, we'd all taken a demotion in title when we were acquired. Group presidents became vice presidents. Vice presidents became general managers. It shouldn't have mattered, because neither our scopes of responsibility nor salaries had changed. But it mattered to me. I liked my old title. It made me feel important.

John didn't make any of us feel important. It soon became apparent he intended to push Jeff aside and have him go the way of his peers. The other group presidents from our former company had all left the corporation. Jeff was the lone holdout. Both John and he had made it abundantly clear Jeff's remaining tenure would be short. At the end of our one of monthly operating reviews, Jeff had commented, "Don't expect me to have a career with this company.

Hell, you shouldn't expect me to be here this time next year."

John, for his part, simply went around Jeff as though he weren't even there. He began having me report various things directly to him.

"Dan, I'm going to need you to start sending me your daily production numbers, so I can monitor your trends."

This gave John almost a daily opportunity to shit all over my team and me as we struggled to recover. It baffled me that John would devote such attention to our business, whose revenues accounted for less than one percent of his entire portfolio. We weren't even material.

And then, on a Thursday, John informed us he'd be visiting the following Tuesday. Jeff was traveling out of the country and would not be present for the visit. That was unusual. Whether by coincidence or design, we'd be facing King John alone.

We ceased all productive activity in the plant and went to General Quarters—the Naval term for battle stations—to prepare for the visit. John had given us a lengthy data-compilation assignment to complete in advance of the visit. I volunteered myself for that. Then we laid out tour routes and designated specific employees to man various points along it. That was a joint effort. Next, we put together a task list to structure our cleaning, decluttering, and organizing effort. Again, most of the team played some part. Then, we put together an outline for the business update we would present during the discussion portion of the agenda. I again volunteered myself to pull it all together. Finally, we drafted a full schedule of events, a down-to-the-minute agenda of John's every movement and activity for the entire duration of his visit. For this, I fell back on my Navy executive assistant experience, having managed similar events for senior officers numerous times in the past.

It was a significant investment of time and effort with little expected return. By the time John arrived, I was proud of the team for getting our business as ready as it possibly could be for the beating it would undoubtedly take.

John wasted no time. Following handshakes and introductions, he began, "Let me start by putting you all at ease. If I wanted to shut this plant down, I wouldn't waste my time coming here. I could do that over the phone. Nobody needs to go find a new job."

Whew! What a relief! Thanks, King John.

The comment was an apparent reference to a recent visit he'd made to a facility that had also had a *footprint rationalization* project foisted upon it and was struggling as a result. There, John had chastised the group for not recovering faster and made comments suggesting the facility's future was very much in question. Not even a week later, key members of the leadership team departed. People who had never considered taking calls from headhunters suddenly did. *Nicely done, King John.*

John apparently didn't want the same to happen in our facility. But following his weak, awkward attempt to reassure us, he immediately departed from our prepared script to thoroughly bash us for our recent financial performance.

"Look at this." John had us all squinting at a small cell on his massive spreadsheet. "You see that? You had the worst cashflow in the entire group!"

Of course we did. We'd been required to spend millions to shut down a plant and move a bunch of equipment, none of which had been our idea. That had succeeded in putting our annual cashflow in the toilet. When our engineering manager pointed this out to John, he just dismissed it.

"To be perfectly clear, from a cashflow perspective, I'm better off without you."

Wow. What happened to the words of reassurance?

No doubt, our financial performance had sucked. But that was due entirely to our ongoing inability to produce and sell product. I had recently made some leadership changes to better align our best talents to meet the challenges of getting healthy. But, as we explained, the best we could hope for were small, incremental improvements until we made investments to properly repair and upgrade the equipment. Without additional resources, no amount of added effort would yield a materially different outcome.

"Investment? Are you kidding me? You have to prove you can *make* money before you can expect to *get* any. And you guys haven't proven you can make money, not even close." Clearly, John wasn't about to open his wallet for us.

The beating continued in the conference room a while longer before we finally moved on to the plant tour. John had made it clear the purpose of his visit had been to deliver a beat-down for our financial performance. That achieved, he seemed completely disinterested in what was happening out on the production floor, visibly forcing himself through the motions of the tour and the various *employee engagement* opportunities we'd put together for him. He was robotic. All the spit-polishing we'd done had apparently been a complete waste of time.

John was far more at ease once Chet and I returned him to his Gulfstream. The King clearly preferred his throne room to the shop floor. It was a terrific relief for all of us when the cabin door finally closed, the engines spun up, and John and his jet taxied out of sight.

Two months later, we got to do it all over again.

Our biggest customer had been demanding a meeting with King John for months. Jeff had succeeded in keeping them at bay, but my own efforts to do the same had failed after Jeff left the company—he'd done so a month after John's visit to our plant. With Jeff gone, there was no one left in the chain of command standing between John and me. The last thing I wanted was for him to get involved, but, ultimately, I couldn't avoid it. I set up a meeting.

The original plan was to conduct the meeting at my facility. But due to a last-minute schedule change, John couldn't spare the time for a return trip to the plant, and we instead decided to meet the customer at the executive airport nearby. This would allow John to do a quick touch-and-go in his Gulfstream. He seemed much happier with this arrangement, and my team and I were thrilled not to have him return to our facility. The customer was happy just to finally get a meeting.

I'd reserved a large conference room at the airport for the meeting. Once we'd all taken our seats around the table, John began the conversation by saying, "I understand we've created some difficulties for you. I regret that."

It was a prompt for our customer to begin airing his grievances. The CEO commenced ticking our many failures off his list and eventually landed on the topic of our supply agreement. We'd put one in place two years prior, and, due to our ongoing struggles to return production to normal levels, had failed to supply the quantities set forth in that agreement for several months.

Struggles aside, the CEO was certain the primary reason for this failure was that we were diverting product that could have gone to his company to an internal customer. In addition to the product we supplied to the open market, we also manufactured goods for other business units within our corporation. These were managed as internal inventory transfers, for which my business made no money. Given the choice, I would have much preferred selling what we made externally. I didn't get a single sales dollar for anything passed internally.

I'd explained this to the CEO numerous times, but he was unconvinced. On more than one occasion, he'd accused us of breaching our supply agreement and suggested that perhaps there were some legal remedy he might pursue. Having been embroiled in two legal disputes, involving decisions made and actions taken well before I'd come long, I had *zero* desire to be dragged into one more. So, I'd treaded very lightly on the subject, underscoring all the actions we'd taken, at great expense to our business, to maximize the product we provided him.

I had forewarned John the CEO might go down this path.

"Let him," had been his response. "I refuse to be bullied."

The CEO explained to John, "So, you see, from our perspective, you're supplying your internal customer with product that should rightfully be ours . . . *legally* be ours."

Seizing upon the implicit threat, John immediately shot back, "Are you suggesting you intend to sue us? Is that what you're saying?"

The CEO's eyes went wide. "No . . . no, no, no. Of course not. I, uh, am just saying that, uh, I want to make sure we're getting our fair share." He was in total retreat.

It was brilliant. By directly confronting the CEO, John had neutered him. And he'd done so calmly, professionally, and matter-of-factly. I was no fan of John's, but I had to acknowledge the beauty of what he'd just achieved. It was one of the most impressive pieces of executive maneuvering I'd ever witnessed. Maybe, just maybe, I could learn something from this guy.

Or not. After the meeting ended, John started for the door to the terminal leading out to the tarmac. He stopped after two steps, turned back to me, and said, "By the way, when you're communicating with a group president, you don't just throw out a bunch of numbers without providing a little context first. Don't make an executive at my level have to guess what he's reading."

John was referring to the email exchange we'd had over the weekend. I had provided him a few slides that had captured the history and current state of our relationship with this customer. Included were recent sales figures for the products we provided. John wanted to know how the gross margin we'd captured on those sales had varied from year to year. Knowing his penchant for numbers and disdain for words, I put together a small table with that data and sent it to him without any additional explanation. All of the context around those numbers was in the presentation I'd provided and the email chain that accompanied it. I thought I'd given him exactly what he wanted.

I got that burning sensation in my ears. Here he was again, the condescending prick.

I unclenched my teeth and replied, "I didn't want to clutter your in-box with a lot of over-explanation, so I just sent the numbers you requested. I'll provide a brief summary to go along with them next time."

He gave me the same, disappointed look he always gave me and forced out a terse, "Thanks."

No, thank you, *King John. And thanks for gracing us with your presence.*

All hail The King!

LESSONS LEARNED

1. Things can change. Fast. You may never see it coming. But don't ever be surprised when it does. Good, bad, or indifferent, things *will* eventually change.

2. Business disruption is never easy, whether a merger, acquisition, facility closure, or relocation. Playbooks are nice, but never provide the complete or final answer. Every situation is unique and presents its own challenges. Don't let anyone tell you otherwise, especially the clowns from corporate.

3. A competent asshole is still an asshole, even if he's effective. It can be miserable working for one. But not as miserable as working for an *in*competent, *in*effective asshole. I would prefer not to work for any assholes. But, if I had to choose, I would take the competent one. Maybe I could at least learn something.

Epilogue

S o where am I now?

Somehow, I wasn't fired. And that surprised me.

As I was driving to the hangar to meet King John, the thought occurred to me, *So . . .* this *is how it's going down.* It was the perfect set-up. The king flies in on his corporate jet, skillfully calls my most problematic customer's bluff, asks me to stay behind as the others file out, and then . . . BAM! He fires me.

Except he didn't. For sure, I'm still a hapless plebe, as far as King John is concerned. But I'm still here. And the team and I even managed to squeeze a few dollars out of him. He authorized the capital investment we needed to upgrade our equipment and get our plant healthy. And we did. Six months after our meeting in the hangar, I informed the king we were finally able to meet our production targets. He congratulated us. Then he left us alone. *Victory!*

Unfortunately, it was too little, too late for our customers. Most of them left us for competitors, including the one whose CEO King John shot a bunch of daylight through that day. After all that drama, they ditched us.

"We're in our slow season," they said. *Yeah, right.*

We still have our challenges. But we're still in the fight.

And a funny thing happened. My experience of the previous decade caught up with me in an unexpected way. Day after day, with bad news following bad news, I caught myself thinking, *Yeah, this seems about right. Things have rarely gone smoothly for me. Why should they now?* And I was entirely at peace, projecting a calmness those around me found reassuring. I could stand at the head of the patrol and not duck at the sound of gunfire.

Without question, I had grown as a leader. I was grateful for that, because I wanted this period in my life to count for something.

Elsewhere, I finally made peace with my decision to leave the Navy.

I didn't bolt upright in bed one morning and declare, "All right! I'm over it!" Rather, I began to feel, more and more, that I was engaged in a worthwhile struggle. It was a struggle to overcome my own idealism and naïveté; a struggle to form my own, unique identity out of uniform; and a struggle to define success in my own terms, and not in comparison to the growing prestige of my over-achieving Annapolis and Harvard classmates. I stopped envying them and started cheering for them. That's a far healthier place to be.

I speak with friends retiring from the Navy, and I think, *Damn, I'm soooo glad that's not me.* I couldn't imagine having to start all over again, not at this age. Yes, I had to learn my lessons the hard way. But I'm glad I did so in the vigor of early adulthood and not in the yawning approach to middle age. I'm not sure I could put up with half the bullshit now as I did when I was thirty.

The United States Navy has been, and always will be, the great joy of my life. I don't expect any civilian experience ever to equal it.

But let's be honest. Being in the military was easy. Being a civilian is hard.

Conclusion

I had a good run in the Navy. I got into Harvard. I carried some unrealistic expectations into the private sector, made some poor choices, and experienced some bad luck. And I learned some important lessons along the way.

So what?

So what? So let's dance!

I think Rodney Dangerfield got it exactly right in *Caddyshack*. To hell with it. Let's party! All any of us can do is strive to live the best life possible, whatever hand we've been dealt.

With that in mind, I leave you with these parting thoughts.

1. You are not alone.

At my personal low point, convinced I was a failure for not living to my full potential, I was fortunate to have had serendipitous encounters with fellow veterans or Harvard Business School graduates who *felt exactly the same way*. What a godsend those conversations were. Everyone's story was a bit different, but I learned I wasn't the only one out there *not* crushing it, despite appearances to the contrary. I wasn't the only one heaping enormous pressure on myself and then engaging in unhealthy self-flagellation for not living up to my own, unrealistic expectations.

I wouldn't wish such an affliction on anyone. But what a relief to learn I wasn't the only one suffering from it.

I get asked for career advice from time to time. People learn of my pedigree and think I know what the hell I'm doing. And often in those conversations, typically with young people just starting their careers, I sense self-doubt. And then I sense guilt for the self-doubt.

"Stop!" I tell them. "You do *not* have to figure out the next fifty years of your life in the next thirty minutes. And that's perfectly okay. There's nothing wrong with you."

Struggling? Haven't figured it all out? That's fine. Neither have I. You are not alone.

2. Don't settle. But don't seek perfection, either.

We're taught that job-hopping is bad. Too many moves in too short a period of time suggests you're a flake. And no one wants to hire a flake.

But gutting it out in a role that's a poor fit can close just as many doors. You under-perform. You're marginalized. You're unhappy, which makes you come across as an asshole. And under-performing, marginalized assholes typically do not promote. You're better off leaving.

The tricky thing is, you don't always know which roles will be the best fit. The job description says one thing. The recruiter says another. The hiring manager says still another. And then you take the job, and your experience bears no resemblance whatsoever to any of the descriptions anyone provided. *Shit.*

Every new opportunity carries risks. And those risks should be borne, smartly, as you work your way to your best-fit role.

That role is a very worthwhile objective. It's your opportunity to spend much of your waking hours as the best, most productive version of yourself. It's your opportunity to achieve success seemingly effortlessly and to have others say, "Wow. She makes it look so easy." It's your opportunity for your boss's peers to fight over you. "Come on, Tom . . . I *have* to have him on this project!"

But it will never be perfect. Even your best-fit role will have undesirable qualities. Meetings you'd rather not attend. People with whom you'd rather not collaborate. Trips you'd rather not take. Conference calls you'd rather not join. Even the job we love carries some things we hate.

Don't settle for less than your best-fit role. But don't seek perfection, either. You'll turn your career into a never-ending series of existential crises that will cost you inordinate time, money, and relationships. Trust me, it isn't worth it.

3. First, be a good boss.

What if there were a Hippocratic Oath for bosses? What if anyone, anywhere, responsible for the productive employment of even a single person, were required to pledge to *first, be a good boss?* Would it somehow stem the current pandemic of shitty bosses?

Most of us spend the majority of our adult lives at work, and bosses therefore have an outsized influence on the quality of our life experience. And that experience can be made miserable by a shitty boss.

A friend once shared a terrific piece of wisdom a mentor had handed down to him: the moment you become someone's boss, you become a nightly topic of conversation at that person's dinner table.

Yikes. You can only imagine how unpleasant such conversations must be these days.

I don't know if I'm a good boss. But I am absolutely determined not to be a shitty one.

To be a good boss does not mean one has a to be a pushover, quite the contrary. Good bosses do what's necessary to get results.

Good bosses aren't in it to make friends.

But there are certain things good bosses do that make them tolerable, even agreeable to those they lead. They're humble. They're supportive. They set clear expectations. They're consistent in thought and deed. And they provide adequate feedback, so employees never need to guess where they stand. Anyone can do these things, but my experience suggests far few do.

I once heard a retired Navy admiral explain his approach to retaining top-performing sailors.

"I was never so arrogant as to think I was the reason they stayed. But I was determined *not* to be the reason they left."

I think that's a great starting point for any boss.

If you have but one direct report, consider it your sacred obligation to *first, be a good boss.*

* * *

Some will read this and think, "What a story! Such perseverance . . ."
Others will read it and think, "What a story! Fucking idiot . . ."
I don't disagree with either.
Thanks for reading.

Acknowledgments

What is *this?*
Without an answer to that question, there could be no book. That's what my friend, Neil Pasricha, bestselling author and Harvard Business School classmate, taught me. And it took me more than five years to figure it out. But it was well worth it. For that, and the for all the sound advice he's provided, I will always be grateful. Thanks, Neil.

Wow. I had no idea you were such an asshole.

It takes a really good friend to call you an asshole. Alexa Maranhao, US Naval Academy Class of 2009, is that friend. And in calling me an asshole, she provided the key insight that pulled this whole thing together. Thanks for that, Alexa, and for suffering through the earliest versions of the manuscript. You're awesome.

How about you get your writing on centerline?

I thought I was a good writer. Actually, I didn't think. I was certain. That is, until David Vickers of IronMule Creative, LLC, informed me otherwise. And he was exactly right. My writing was lacking, in so many ways. But David provided me the tools with which to fix it, as well as the motivation to get off my ass and finally get this thing done. Thank you, David.

I think you've got something here.

You write you something. You love it. And you hope others will, too. But you can't be sure. My sister, Ann Bozung Tormoen, is the straightest of straight shooters. If she thought it sucked, she'd tell me. When she said she liked it, I knew I had something. Thanks, Ann.

The same goes for Justin Schmitt. Ann introduced me to him. Justin was the first non-friend or family remember to see the manuscript. I knew he, too, would give it to me straight. He broke the manuscript down like Norm Abram would an antique chest of drawers. He provided thoughtful, incredibly useful feedback. And loads of encouragement. Much appreciated, Justin.

That son of a bitch! I used to work for that guy!

My brother-in-law, Zeb Hill, spent no time in the military. But he's spent too much time under the thumb of a shitty boss. His visceral reaction to the manuscript, and the unfortunate ease with which he identified with its characters, convinced me to soldier on. Thanks, Zeb.

We like your book. But don't let that go to your head, Navy!

It's one thing for friends and family to like your book. But it's entirely another for a publisher to do so. John Koehler and his team saw potential in these pages and in me as a writer. Yes, that can quickly go to your head. But not on John's watch. The publication process can be daunting . . . and loads of fun. For me, it was far more the latter than the former. Thanks, John. And Go Navy!

Elsewhere, legions have lent a sympathetic ear through the years as I've whined about my never-ending parade of shitty bosses and jobs. Those include Cliff Adams, Terry Bassham, Ron and Donna Bozung, Adam Brock, Andy Byers, Bill Dwyer, Sam Furlong, Jason Gibson, Chris Jividen, Ben Jones, Vice Admiral (retired) Joe Leidig, Bruce and Pearl MacDonald, Mark Nevitt, Tamin Pechet, Mike Petersen, JJ Puga, Joe Reniers, Mark Russ, Kristy Schultz, Dave

Traugott, Keith White, and numerous others. Sorry you had to listen to all that. And thank you for doing so.

Finally, writing this was cathartic. But it was little consolation for Tricia and Alex, my wife and daughter, who had to put up with me through this whole civilian experience. I was impossible. And I am truly sorry. I love you both very much.

CPSIA information can be obtained
at www.ICGtesting.com
Printed in the USA
LVHW091359230920
666891LV00003B/862

9 781646 631520